Oh Gussie!

Oh Gussie!

Cooking *and* Visiting *in* Kimberly's Southern Kitchen

KIMBERLY SCHLAPMAN

WITH MARTHA FOOSE

WM

WILLIAM MORROW
An Imprint of HarperCollins Publishers

HarperCollins books may be purchased for educational, business, or sales promotional use. For information please e-mail the Special Markets Department at SPsales@harpercollins.com.

FIRST EDITION

Designed by Kris Tobiassen of Matchbook Digital
Photography by beall + thomas photography, except
for images on pages 17 and 224 by the Photographix

Library of Congress Cataloging-in-Publication Data has been applied for.

ISBN 978-0-06-232371-2

15 16 17 18 19   OV/QG   10 9 8 7 6 5 4 3 2 1

To my mama and daddy

I learned from the best. There are no two more loving and lovable parents! Mama is the greatest cook I know and taught me how to take care of the people I love through cooking for them. Daddy happily tasted every single dish we ever made—the good, the bad, and the scorched!

And in memory of my brother-in-law Allen Schlapman

who absolutely loved gathering around the table with family.
We miss you, Allen.

You will show me the path of life;
in Your presence is fullness of joy; at
Your right hand are pleasures forevermore.

—Psalms 16:11

I just believe in putting kindness into the universe.

—Emmylou Harris

Contents

INTRODUCTION

I've been cooking as long as I've been singing, which is simply as long as I can remember. Singing in church and sitting counterside helping my mama and grand-mothers cook taught me a lot about life. Those ladies were at the door of anyone around who had a birth or death in their family, got a promotion, lost a job, or just broke a bone—with some kind of casserole or cake in hand and with me and my little sister in tow.

Aside from learning to cook, I learned how important it is to share time in the kitchen with people you love, to nourish your family, and to foster friendships. Our families' kitchens were where I found my passion and my voice.

I love to see real emotion on people's faces as I sing a song. I adore hearing the pleasure in people's voices when I have cooked something that brings great delight to their taste buds or comfort to their hearts.

Growing up in the Appalachian foothills of North Georgia, we were taught to love simple pleasures, like Sunday rides in the country, a warm cobbler, the sound of children singing. Those are the things I remember from my childhood, and they still make me happy today. I like to take care of people, make people happy. I find such pleasure in filling up bellies!

My home is where my heart is, and my kitchen is the heart of my home. It's where I take care of people. My desire is for you to show love to the people who mean the most to you through the recipes in this book. I am sharing my heart in the stories and memories that I hold most dear. I hope they spark memories in you and inspire you to love even deeper with every dusting of flour and tearful chopping of onions.

Oh Gussie!

CHAPTER 1

Family

I come from a mixture of one-quarter old Hollywood glamour and three-quarters hardworking, God-fearing country roots. I attribute my slight addiction to stilettos and shiny frocks, along with a bit of my mischievous nature, to my Grandmother Burrell, on my mama's side. She grew up in a well-to-do household in Beverly Hills, California, dining out at The Brown Derby. She fell head over heels for my charmingly Southern grandfather from the hills of North Georgia. Papa Burrell had had a hard life and grew up working for every penny he was afforded. He even had to quit school as a boy to go to work.

My mama's folks met at a dime store in California when my Papa Burrell was stationed out west in the Army. He told his buddy right then and there, "Now, that's the girl I am going to marry." They fell fast and were married. After using up his furlough days, he even went AWOL to extend their visit to Georgia to see his parents. Since it was wartime and he was being sent to Hawaii, his forgiving superior officer turned a blind eye to the offense. He spent four years in the Army, where he served under the great General Patton and was awarded two Bronze Stars. I would sit, all ears, as Grandmother Burrell retold the hysterically romantic story of getting off the train in Georgia, walking far up the dirt road in her stilettos, and losing a heel on her way to meet her new family. She was a reverse Beverly Hillbilly! She came to the South with no experience at all in the kitchen—why, the first time she cooked corn for her husband, to her surprise it turned into popcorn right there in the pan! But she transformed into a brilliant homemaker.

On my daddy's side of the family, my Papa Bramlett met Grandmother Bramlett at a friend's birthday party in Demorest, Georgia. They were secretly married when she was sixteen. Her daddy did not want her to marry that young, so they snuck off to Walhalla, South Carolina, where you can still get married today if you're sixteen. I always thought that was so incredibly romantic! They were so very sweet. Papa was a farmer. He grew vegetables and drove them over two hours to sell at the farmers' market in Atlanta. Papa sang in a men's quartet and had the most charming welcome: when anyone would walk in the house, he would sweetly sing hello—I still hear his melodic greeting and even use his welcome a lot myself! Grandmother and he lived on a farm, where they would give us kids truckbed rides through the pasture on Sunday afternoons. There was a rickety old bridge over the creek that we swore was always about to give way, and we'd hold our breath every time we crossed it. He never worried, though. He drove over that thing like it was built of steel! My grandmother is one of the most loving people I know. She taught me to forgo hand-shaking and to just go on in for the hug. She exudes love and mercy. Her philosophy is "The more, the merrier—we can always make more biscuits!" We recently celebrated my dear Grandmother Bramlett's ninety-first birthday. I'm so grateful to still have her in my life. Her father, interestingly enough, also traveled with a gospel quartet. I think both those fine tenors would've really gotten a kick out of our band!

My parents met at school in Cornelia, Georgia. My daddy was a rough, mischievous yet adorable rascal, a bit like his own daddy. My mama was a prim, proper angel just like her mama. When she and my daddy started dating, she would make him call her as soon as he got home after their dates, not trusting him to go straight home. She clipped his wings a little, and that thrilled his mother and sisters, who constantly worried about his safety. My daddy's whole family fell in love with his gal! My folks married young and had me first. Five years later, my sister, Paula, came along. I adored her instantly! Paula and I got along great. We never fought, and still to this day we don't fight. She's my best friend. But we did get ourselves into trouble a great deal. We joke that she and I just about killed one of the peach trees that used to grow in the yard because of all the switches that had to be taken from it to set us straight!

When I was seventeen, I went off to college to study music in Birmingham, Alabama. When my parents took me back to school after Christmas of my freshman year, they stopped at a pharmacy and, unbeknownst to me, bought a pregnancy test. They bought the test there in Birmingham because had they bought it in our small-town pharmacy, folks would have thought it was for me! Nope! Mama was forty-one and had a baby on the way! In those days, a forty-one-year-old pregnant woman might as well have been Abraham's wife, Sarah. My brother, Joshua, was born when I was nineteen. He was incredibly cute, and we spoiled him rotten. I can't imagine what our family would be like today if it hadn't been for that little surprise.

Grandmother Bramlett was a wonderful cooking teacher, and Josh used to sit on the counter to watch her cook. He especially loved to watch her make breakfast in the morning. Once when he spent the night with her and Papa, he walked into my grandparents' room the next morning and announced, "Breakfast is ready! Don't know how to make coffee." That little fellow had cooked an entire breakfast! He was only five years old!

The dishes in this chapter are dishes we have shared in our family for years. Some I have tweaked a touch, and others I would not change for a million dollars.

GOLDEN DELICIOUS COLESLAW

My uncle David loves pepper jelly! Whenever I come for a visit he foists his latest pepper jelly find on me. It has gotten to be a running joke between us. Try this slaw dressing with your favorite pepper jelly. I always look for interesting batches at roadside stands and farmers' markets. No two batches may ever be alike, but the slaw is always bound to be good! This colorful slaw combines mellow Golden Delicious apple matchsticks with a flare of hot pepper.

Makes 6 servings

2 CUPS THINLY SLICED GREEN CABBAGE

1 ¼ CUPS THINLY SLICED RED CABBAGE

1 LARGE CARROT, SHREDDED

2 GOLDEN DELICIOUS APPLES, PEELED, CORED, AND CUT INTO MATCHSTICKS

1 CUP MAYONNAISE

3 TABLESPOONS APPLE CIDER VINEGAR

¼ CUP APPLE HABANERO PEPPER JELLY (TEXAS PEPPER JELLY)

SALT AND FRESHLY GROUND BLACK PEPPER

Combine the cabbage, carrot, apples, mayonnaise, vinegar, and jelly in a large bowl and mix well to incorporate. Season with salt and pepper to taste. Cover and refrigerate for at least 1 hour.

SOUTHERN SIMPLE: This is a great make-ahead recipe. It needs to sit for at least an hour so the juices get released. The apple and veggies become a little soft but still have a nice crunch to them.

It the slaw is going to sit for an extended time, toss the apple matchsticks in vinegar to keep them from turning brown.

SOUTHERN SIMPLE: If you can't find apple pepper jelly at the market, substitute 2 tablespoons hot pepper jelly and 2 tablespoons apple jelly for the apple habanero jelly.

SOUTHERN MOTHER: A sweet hostess gift is a jar of apple habanero pepper jelly from my buddies over in Texas, tied up with a recipe card for this slaw. You can order their wonderful jelly at www.texaspepperjelly.com.

LAYERED SALAD

This colorful salad is a perfect "make 'n' take" for a picnic or potluck, and it's one of the recipes I turn to when I get together with my sister, sister-in-law, and cousins. Once it's all layered up, the salad can hang out in the fridge while I hang out with my girls!

Makes 8 servings

2 HEADS ROMAINE LETTUCE, SHREDDED

4 CUPS CHOPPED TOMATOES

2 CUPS FINELY CHOPPED RED ONION

ONE 16-OUNCE BAG FROZEN PEAS, THAWED

1 CUP MAYONNAISE

1 TABLESPOON SUGAR

2 TEASPOONS SALT

2 TABLESPOONS CHOPPED FRESH DILL

1½ CUPS SHREDDED CHEDDAR CHEESE

6 SLICES BACON, COOKED AND CRUMBLED

Layer the lettuce, tomatoes, red onions, and peas in a large glass bowl. Mix the mayonnaise, sugar, salt, and dill in a small bowl. Spread the mayonnaise mixture evenly on top of the peas. Finish with layers of Cheddar and bacon. Cover with plastic wrap and refrigerate for at least 1 hour. Toss before serving.

SOUTHERN SIMPLE: To punch up this salad for a speedy weeknight meal, add a layer of leftover diced cooked chicken or ham. Cooked salad-size shrimp makes a nice addition, too.

SOUTHERN SKINNY: Use fat-free mayonnaise and substitute turkey bacon and reduced-fat shredded cheese to trim a few calories off this salad.

CUCUMBER TEA SANDWICHES

These petite finger sandwiches have been a favorite of mine since I was a little girl. We always seemed to serve them on happy occasions, most of the time with only the ladies for baby or bridal showers, graduation teas, and luncheons. I remember Mama getting up early on Saturday mornings when she had a shower or meeting to go to and making these little goodies. I especially remember her carefully trimming the ends off the bread.

Makes 24 tea sandwiches

8 OUNCES CREAM CHEESE, AT ROOM TEMPERATURE

1 CUP SEEDED AND GRATED CUCUMBER

¼ CUP FINELY CHOPPED SCALLIONS

2 TABLESPOONS MAYONNAISE

1 TABLESPOON HOT SAUCE

SALT AND FRESHLY GROUND BLACK PEPPER

24 SLICES WHITE BREAD

1. Mix the cream cheese, cucumber, scallions, mayonnaise, and hot sauce in a small bowl. Season with salt and pepper to taste.

2. Spread an even layer of the cheese mixture on 12 slices of bread. Top each with the other pieces of bread to make 12 sandwiches. Trim the crusts off all the sandwiches, then slice each diagonally into 2 triangular tea sandwiches. Arrange them on a platter.

SOUTHERN SIMPLE: You can make these sandwiches ahead, but be sure to cover them with a damp paper towel and plastic wrap or the bread will start to dry up and curl at the edges.

SOUTHERN SIMPLE: To seed and grate the cucumbers, slice them lengthwise, then use a spoon to scrape out and discard the seeds. Grate the cucumber flesh using a box grater. If using English cucumbers, there is no need to seed.

SOUTHERN SKINNY: To lighten this recipe, use ⅓-less-fat cream cheese (Neufchâtel) and fat-free mayonnaise or reduced-fat Vegenaise on thin-sliced low-calorie bread.

Papa's Peaches and Cottage Cheese

My daddy's daddy loved peaches and cottage cheese. I created this dish with him in mind. It is wonderful just about any time of day but particularly delicious for breakfast. The peaches can be sweetened the night before and refrigerated while the nuts can be spiced and baked ahead of time, ready to go in the morning.

Makes 4 servings

3 PEACHES, PEELED, PITTED, AND ROUGHLY CHOPPED

2 TABLESPOONS PLUS ¼ CUP SUGAR

1 EGG WHITE

1 TABLESPOON WATER

½ TEASPOON GROUND CINNAMON

¼ TEASPOON SALT

1 CUP PECAN HALVES

2 CUPS COTTAGE CHEESE

1. Preheat the oven to 350°F. Line a baking sheet with parchment paper.

2. Toss the peaches with 2 tablespoons sugar in a large bowl. Let the peaches macerate at room temperature for at least 30 minutes and up to 1 hour to release the juices.

3. Meanwhile, whisk the egg white and water in a bowl until foamy. Add the remaining ¼ cup sugar, the cinnamon, and salt and whisk until the mixture is thick and opaque. Add the pecans and stir to coat thoroughly. Transfer the nuts to the prepared baking sheet, using a fork to space out the pecans and get rid of any excess egg white coating. (Discard the remaining coating.)

4. Bake the nuts, stirring every 5 minutes, until deep golden brown, 20 to 25 minutes. Cool completely on the baking sheet.

5. Spoon ½ cup cottage cheese into each of 4 bowls. Top with the peaches and spiced pecans.

SOUTHERN SIMPLE: The spiced pecans can be made up to 4 days ahead. Store the nuts in an airtight container at room temperature. The recipe doubles easily, and these sweet, spicy nuts are great to have on hand as an addition to a salad or just for snacking.

SOUTHERN MOTHER: This is a sweet way to get a bit of calcium and protein plus a serving of fruit to start the day.

New Bride's Vegetable Beef Soup

When I was a new bride at twenty-one, my Grandmother Burrell mailed me this recipe. She had written it on little lined notepaper. I think she figured if I could make a good pot of soup I might do all right as a homemaker and wife. She was right. This one's easy, forgiving, and impressive—just like a good marriage!

Makes 6 servings

1 POUND GROUND BEEF

1 SMALL ONION, CHOPPED (ABOUT ¾ CUP)

TWO 10.75-OUNCE CANS CONDENSED TOMATO SOUP

2 SMALL RUSSET (BAKING) POTATOES, PEELED AND CUT INTO MEDIUM DICE (ABOUT 2 CUPS)

ONE 15-OUNCE CAN SLICED CARROTS, DRAINED AND RINSED, OR 2 CUPS CHOPPED FRESH CARROTS

ONE 15-OUNCE CAN GREEN BEANS, DRAINED AND RINSED, OR 2 CUPS FROZEN GREEN BEANS

ONE 15-OUNCE CAN WHOLE KERNEL CORN, DRAINED AND RINSED, OR 2 CUPS FROZEN CORN

ONE 16-OUNCE CAN NAVY BEANS, DRAINED AND RINSED

ONE 14.5-OUNCE CAN DICED TOMATOES

SALT AND FRESHLY GROUND BLACK PEPPER

1 TABLESPOON CHOPPED FRESH PARSLEY

1 TABLESPOON CHOPPED FRESH OREGANO

1 TABLESPOON CHOPPED FRESH BASIL

1. Cook the ground beef in a large stockpot over medium heat until it starts to turn brown, about 3 minutes.

2. Drain the fat from the pot. Add the onion and cook until softened, about 5 minutes. Stir in the tomato soup. Fill each can with water and add it to the pot. Add the potatoes, carrots, green beans, corn, navy beans, and tomatoes. Season with salt and pepper to taste. Bring the soup to a boil, then reduce the heat to low, cover, and simmer for 40 minutes.

3. Just before serving, stir in the fresh herbs. Season with more salt and pepper if needed.

SOUTHERN SIMPLE: Some days around our house more people drop over than expected at dinnertime. When that happens, you can add one 8-ounce package of egg noodles to make this recipe go further. Cook the noodles according to the instructions on the package.

SOUTHERN MOTHER: One day when my daughter sets up housekeeping as a new bride, I'll mail her this recipe from my grandmother.

I'm a sucker for romance, and I have sung for more weddings than I can count. It's always cool to watch those moments from a special perspective. I am usually positioned in the front of the church or chapel very close to the action. I must say one of my most memorable moments was while I was singing "The Lord's Prayer" at the Cornelia First United Methodist Church. I was probably sixteen. My friend and organist Bill Loyd and I were doing a classical rendition of this very reverent song, and as I reached the climax, the bride's little brother very quietly fell out! He fainted! I was standing on a platform right over him! Now, that was a first! What to do? There was a bit of a commotion, but Bill and I kept going—the show must go on! Bill recently reminded me that I leaned over to him when the song was over to cautiously ask, "Is he dead?" I know the mother of the bride could have fainted, too!

LINDA'S POTATO SOUP

My sister-in-law Linda is a get-down-to-business kind of gal. She shared this creamy, easy-to-make potato soup recipe with me. The potatoes cook down to thicken the soup, then when it's just about ready, you stir in a whole pint of whipping cream! It's simply wonderful—and always a hit on a cool winter night.

Makes 16 cups (8 to 10 servings)

1 ONION, FINELY CHOPPED

6 CARROTS, FINELY CHOPPED

3 CELERY STALKS, CHOPPED

8 POTATOES, PEELED AND CUT INTO 1-INCH CHUNKS

8 TABLESPOONS (1 STICK) BUTTER

5 CHICKEN BOUILLON CUBES

1 TABLESPOON SALT

¾ TEASPOON FRESHLY GROUND BLACK PEPPER

2 CUPS HEAVY (WHIPPING) CREAM

1 TABLESPOON CHOPPED FRESH PARSLEY

1. Combine the onion, carrots, celery, potatoes, butter, bouillon cubes, salt, and pepper in a large stockpot and add water to cover by 1 inch. Bring to a boil over medium-high heat, then reduce the heat to medium-low and simmer, stirring occasionally, until the vegetables are tender, about 50 minutes. The potatoes will fall apart and thicken the soup.

2. Add the cream and parsley and cook for 10 more minutes, or until creamy and thick. Season with salt and pepper to taste and serve.

> **SOUTHERN SIMPLE:** When I serve this soup for a party, I like to set up a little row of bowls with classic loaded-baked-potato toppings—you know, shredded Cheddar cheese, crumbled bacon, chopped chives, and so on.

> **SOUTHERN MOTHER:** For a filling lunch on the go, in the morning fill a Thermos with hot water while you reheat some of this soup. Pour out the water, then pour your soup into the Thermos. It will stay nice and warm until lunchtime.

MANLY MAN BRUNSWICK STEW

This is a take on Brunswick stew, the classic hearty pot of stew that originated either in Brunswick County, Virginia, or Brunswick, Georgia—depending on who you ask. Back in the day, squirrel and rabbit found their way into the pot. These days, I use a combination of beef and chicken seasoned with a bit of barbecue sauce. This recipe is a favorite of my brother Josh's and his father-in-law, Jeff, two of the manliest men I know. Together they can cook up a pot of this big enough to serve a starving army—and they usually do!

Makes 6 to 8 servings

½ POUND BEEF STEW MEAT

½ POUND BONELESS, SKINLESS CHICKEN THIGHS

1 CUP MEDIUM-DICED RED POTATOES

1 LARGE CARROT, HALVED LENGTHWISE AND SLICED CROSSWISE INTO HALF-MOONS

1 SMALL ONION, CHOPPED (ABOUT ¾ CUP)

ONE 14.5-OUNCE CAN WHOLE KERNEL CORN, DRAINED AND RINSED

TWO 14.5-OUNCE CANS DICED TOMATOES

½ CUP HONEY BARBECUE SAUCE

½ CUP KETCHUP

1 TABLESPOON WORCESTERSHIRE SAUCE

¼ CUP BEEF BROTH

¼ TEASPOON CAYENNE PEPPER

1 BAY LEAF

Combine all the ingredients in a slow cooker. Stir well, cover, and cook on HIGH for 8 hours, or until the beef is tender.

SOUTHERN SIMPLE: I like to cut up all the vegetables the night before. Then in the morning all I have to do is dump the ingredients in the old slow cooker and slap on the lid. When the day is done, so is dinner.

STEWED SUMMER SQUASH

We have great neighbors who share the wealth of their garden. A bit of cream added toward the end of the cooking time in this recipe brings the tender, sweet summer squash and herbs together beautifully.

Makes 4 servings

2 TABLESPOONS OLIVE OIL

1 MEDIUM ONION, CHOPPED

4 CUPS (½-INCH-THICK) SUMMER SQUASH ROUNDS

½ TEASPOON SUGAR

SALT AND FRESHLY GROUND BLACK PEPPER

2 TABLESPOONS BUTTER

2 TABLESPOONS HEAVY (WHIPPING) CREAM

1 TABLESPOON FINELY CHOPPED FRESH CHIVES

1 TABLESPOON FINELY CHOPPED FRESH BASIL

Heat the olive oil in a large skillet over medium heat. Add the onion and cook until softened, about 5 minutes. Add the squash, sprinkle with the sugar, and season with salt and pepper to taste. Cook, stirring, until the squash is slightly tender, about 5 minutes. Add the butter, cover, and cook until the squash is tender, about 10 minutes. Add the cream, chives, and basil and cook until the squash is very tender but not mushy, about 5 minutes. Remove from the heat and let the squash rest, uncovered, for 5 to 7 minutes. The sauce will come together and coat the squash in velvety goodness.

SOUTHERN SIMPLE: This stewed squash is a wonderful side dish for a dinner featuring Pork Tenderloin with Slow-Cooked Applesauce (page 38).

SOUTHERN SIMPLE: I like to keep shelf-stable heavy cream in the pantry for when I need just a splash, as in this creamy stewed squash recipe.

OKRA HASH

There's been a lot of talk lately about the health benefits of coconut oil, so I've been giving it a whirl in the kitchen. It's quickly become a staple in my pantry. Refined coconut oil is mild-tasting, with a slightly tropical flavor, and it can take a higher heat than olive oil when sautéing or frying, which is helpful in this recipe.

Okra is high in fiber and potassium. It's also awfully hard to sneak past some kids. This colorful, nutritious hash uses the buddy system and pairs it with sweet potatoes and sweet peppers to give it a bit more kid appeal.

Makes 4 servings

2 TABLESPOONS REFINED COCONUT OIL

½ CUP FINELY CHOPPED ONION

2 CUPS PEELED AND FINELY DICED SWEET POTATO

3 CUPS (¼-INCH-THICK) SLICES OKRA

½ CUP FINELY CHOPPED RED BELL PEPPER

½ CUP FINELY CHOPPED YELLOW BELL PEPPER

½ TEASPOON SMOKED PAPRIKA

SALT AND FRESHLY GROUND BLACK PEPPER

Heat the olive oil in a large skillet over medium heat. Add the onion and cook, stirring, until translucent, about 2 minutes. Add the sweet potatoes, cover, and cook for 5 minutes. Add the okra, bell peppers, and smoked paprika and cook uncovered until the sweet potatoes are tender, 10 to 12 minutes. Do not stir for the last 6 to

When you've got hair like mine, you are always on the lookout for a good conditioner. Sometimes I just look in the pantry—I use some of that coconut oil to tame these tresses!

When I was a little girl, my Papa Bramlett was a hog farmer, so we always had large tin containers of lard around. Mama would store them in the attic. One hot summer day, she was getting something out of the attic, and I was right under her feet on the attic stairs. One of those large tins of lard fell out, spilling all over my head and giving me the conditioning treatment of my life! Come to think of it, why do I spend so much money on expensive hair products these days when I could do it the "old-school" way?

8 minutes of cooking so that a bit of brown crust forms on the hash. Season with salt and pepper to taste.

SOUTHERN SIMPLE: You can substitute frozen okra right from the freezer in place of the fresh okra; just cook it a minute or two more, if needed.

Donna Schlapman's Corn Casserole

When I was writing this book, my husband said if he could pick just one recipe to add, it would be his mother's corn casserole. She was gracious enough to share the recipe.

When you get married, you marry into a family. I was lucky enough to fall in love with not just my husband, but his family as well. Donna, my mother-in-law, is an elegant lady—and the consummate hostess. She's known for her gracious entertaining, and I've learned so much from her. Why, days before a sit-down dinner, she'll have already assembled all the dishes, glassware, flatware, and linens. She entertains with such poise and grace, and when we host a dinner party, I try to channel my "Inner Donna." One of the main things I've learned from her is to do all you can ahead of time. A flustered hostess can ruin a perfectly good dinner party! So I turn to her corn casserole again and again when cooking for company. Everyone loves this sweet corn custard topped with crispy crumbs, so it's one less thing to worry about.

This casserole is also a Schlapman family favorite. It's just not Thanksgiving without it! Thanksgiving is a bittersweet time for us now. For years it has been the tradition for both sides of our family to make the trek to Nashville to spend Thanksgiving with us. We have a houseful for a week and have a big old time. On the day before Thanksgiving 2012, Allen and his mom and daughter had driven over from Virginia. He took our motorcycle out for a drive and was killed by a drunk driver. That day changed all of our lives forever. My husband founded an organization, The Dogwood Project, in his brother's memory. Its purpose is to help children through the grief of losing a parent or sibling. The Dogwood Project sends a dogwood tree to the grieving child for them to plant in memory of their loved one, and helps the family find counseling for the child. I'm so proud of my husband for the work he has done through The Dogwood Project out of love for his brother. More information can be found at www.thedogwoodproject.org.

Makes 6 servings

TWO 16-OUNCE PACKAGES FROZEN CREAM-STYLE CORN

2 EGGS, BEATEN

¼ CUP SUGAR

6 TABLESPOONS UNSALTED BUTTER, MELTED

1 CUP HEAVY (WHIPPING) CREAM

2 CUPS SALTINE CRACKER CRUMBS

1 TEASPOON SALT

1. Preheat the oven to 350°F.

2. In a large bowl, combine the corn, eggs, sugar, 2 tablespoons of the melted butter, the cream, 1 cup of the cracker crumbs, and the salt. Pour the mixture into a 2-quart baking dish and bake for 15 minutes.

3. Meanwhile, make the topping: In a medium bowl, mix the remaining 1 cup cracker crumbs and the remaining 4 tablespoons melted butter.

4. Spread the topping over the casserole and bake until the topping is nicely browned, about 30 minutes.

SOUTHERN SIMPLE: This casserole can be assembled well ahead of time and refrigerated until ready to bake.

SOUTHERN SIMPLE: In the summer I like to add a tablespoon of chopped fresh basil to the corn mixture, while in the fall I like to add a couple of teaspoons of chopped fresh sage.

Simply Southern Fried Chicken

People get all worked up about fried chicken. That's just the way it is. I like my fried chicken the way my grandmother Bramlett made it—simple. I don't need a lot of hoopla! Taking the one extra step (which really does make a difference) of brining the chicken overnight produces the most tender, moist fried chicken. Save the "eleven herbs and spices" for something else. When it comes to fried chicken, just keep it simple with salt and black pepper.

Makes 4 servings

¾ CUP KOSHER SALT, PLUS MORE TO TASTE

ONE 3- TO 5-POUND WHOLE CHICKEN, CUT INTO 8 PIECES

FRESHLY GROUND BLACK PEPPER

ALL-PURPOSE FLOUR, FOR DREDGING

COCONUT OIL, FOR DEEP-FRYING

1. In a large deep bowl or large stockpot, mix the ¾ cup salt in 1 gallon water until the salt dissolves. Place the chicken pieces in the salted water. You can use a plate as a weight to submerge the chicken in the brine if needed. Cover with plastic wrap and refrigerate at least 2 hours or overnight.

2. Remove the chicken from the brine and dry it very well with paper towels. (Discard the brine.) Season the chicken with salt and pepper. Dredge the chicken pieces in the flour and let them rest for 10 to 15 minutes at room temperature.

3. In the meantime, heat coconut oil in a large cast-iron skillet over medium heat to 350°F. When melted, the oil should reach halfway up the pan.

4. Working in batches so that the chicken has enough room to cook, carefully place the pieces of chicken in the hot oil. Fry on both sides until browned, crispy, and cooked through: The wings and breasts should take 10 to 12 minutes, and the thighs and legs should take 15 to 20 minutes. The internal temperature of the chicken should always be around 180°F. Remove from the pan and drain on paper towels.

SOUTHERN SIMPLE: If you're a novice chicken fryer, cook your light meat and dark meat in separate batches, and use a meat thermometer. There's just nothing worse than biting into a crispy, browned piece of chicken only to find it underdone. The internal temperature for the chicken should read around 180°F when done.

(continued)

SOUTHERN MOTHER: I like cold fried chicken. My grandmother Bramlett seemed to always have a plate of fried chicken covered in wrinkly tin foil in her icebox. Sometimes I'll stash a drumstick in the refrigerator for a secret snack later.

MAKE-AHEAD CHICKEN AND RICE

Some afternoons when nothing is going on, I'll make up this casserole and pop it in the freezer. My mother worked for thirty years as a schoolteacher, and she's quite organized. When I was growing up she always had just the right thing to pull out of the freezer, something she'd planned ahead. So I try to do as she taught me: don't waste time, think ahead about what you need to do. I'm grateful for such a good example. Now when the inevitable flight delay happens, I smile and think to myself, At least supper is almost ready.

Makes 6 servings

ONE 6-OUNCE BOX UNCLE BEN'S LONG GRAIN AND WILD RICE ORIGINAL RECIPE, PREPARED

2½ CUPS DICED COOKED CHICKEN

ONE 14.5-OUNCE CAN FRENCH-STYLE GREEN BEANS, DRAINED AND RINSED

1 CUP DICED CELERY

1 CARROT, FINELY CHOPPED

ONE 10.75-OUNCE CAN CONDENSED CREAM OF CELERY SOUP

½ CUP MAYONNAISE

ONE 4-OUNCE JAR PIMENTOS, DRAINED AND DICED

ONE 5-OUNCE JAR WATER CHESTNUTS, DRAINED, RINSED, AND ROUGHLY CHOPPED

1 TEASPOON SALT

¼ TEASPOON FRESHLY GROUND BLACK PEPPER

8 TABLESPOONS (1 STICK) BUTTER

1 CUP RITZ CRACKER CRUMBS (FROM 1 SLEEVE, ABOUT 31 CRACKERS)

1. Preheat the oven to 350°F. Grease a 9 x 13-inch baking dish.

2. In a large bowl, combine the cooked rice, chicken, green beans, celery, carrot, celery soup, mayonnaise, pimentos, water chestnuts, salt, and pepper. Mix well and pour into the prepared baking dish.

3. Bake until golden brown, about 35 minutes.

4. Meanwhile, melt the butter in a medium pan over low heat. Add the crushed crackers, stirring to coat.

5. Remove the baking dish from the oven and spread the topping over the casserole. Bake for another 15 minutes or until golden brown.

(continued)

SOUTHERN MOTHER: When I want to refrigerate or freeze this casserole, I'll mix the butter-crumb topping and place it in a snack-size zip-top bag and freeze it along with the casserole, all wrapped up with instructions on how to bake it. Then if my hubby or sitter is manning the kitchen in my absence, they'll know just what to do.

KIMBERLY'S CHICKEN AND DUMPLINGS

My mama appeared on my cooking show, Kimberly's Simply Southern, *the very first season it was on the air. She brought out the big old ceramic mixing bowl she always uses to mix up her biscuits and dumplings. It's my grandmother's and has been in our family for seventy-five years. I was so happy to be able to share a family tradition.*

It was finally my turn to make the dumplings. While watching the show months after it was filmed, I saw that Mama made an imperceptible (to all but her daughter) shudder when I added chopped jalapeño to the chicken. She liked it, though, and while it wasn't "her" chicken and dumplings, the torch had been passed. So it's officially now "my" turn to make the chicken and dumplings . . . except when I go home to visit Mama. There's no getting any better than the way she does 'em!

Makes 6 servings

4 BONE-IN, SKIN-ON CHICKEN BREAST HALVES

SALT AND FRESHLY GROUND BLACK PEPPER

ALL-PURPOSE FLOUR, FOR DREDGING

2 TABLESPOONS VEGETABLE OIL

1 MEDIUM ONION, FINELY CHOPPED

½ CUP FINELY CHOPPED CARROT

½ CUP FINELY CHOPPED CELERY

2 JALAPEÑOS, SEEDED AND FINELY CHOPPED

¼ TEASPOON CAYENNE PEPPER

1 TABLESPOON FINELY CHOPPED FRESH THYME

6 CUPS CHICKEN BROTH

3 CUPS SELF-RISING FLOUR

3 TABLESPOONS VEGETABLE SHORTENING

¾ TO 1 CUP COLD MILK

½ CUP HEAVY (WHIPPING) CREAM

1. Season the chicken with salt and pepper. Dredge in all-purpose flour.

2. Heat the oil in a large Dutch oven over medium heat. Add the chicken, skin side down, and cook until browned, about 3 minutes. Turn the chicken over and brown the other side. Remove the chicken to a platter.

3. Add the onion, carrot, celery, jalapeños, cayenne, and thyme to the pot. Stir and cook until the onion is softened, about 5 minutes. Return the browned chicken to

the pot and add the chicken stock. Bring to a boil, then reduce the heat to low and simmer for 20 minutes.

4. Meanwhile, make the dumpling dough. In a large bowl, mix the self-rising flour and shortening until crumbly, then add ¾ cup milk. Using your hands, knead the dough until it is firm and holds its shape. Add a bit more milk if it's too dry. Knead it a few times to make it come together. Cover with plastic wrap and set aside.

5. Remove the cooked chicken from the pot and let it cool for a few minutes. Remove the skin and bones and discard. Using 2 forks, shred the chicken, then put it back in the pot. Stir in the heavy cream.

6. On a floured surface (flour the rolling pin as well), roll out the dough to a ¼-inch thickness. Cut it into strips about 1 inch wide, then cut the strips into 2-inch pieces. Carefully drop the dumplings into the pot. Cover halfway with a lid and simmer until the dumplings are tender, about 20 minutes. Season with salt and pepper to taste.

SOUTHERN SIMPLE: Make everything except the dumpling dough ahead of time and reheat the shredded chicken and stock while you make the dumplings.

An ongoing family tease for my mama began one Sunday at my home in Nashville when the whole family was together for Sunday dinner. We were all at the table anxiously awaiting Mama's famous chicken and dumplings. We gathered hands, said the blessing, and began passing the dumplings around the table. Usually the next thing you hear is everybody going crazy with yummy noises. MMMmms and yummms. This time there was total silence until my always-honest brother-in-law Brian broke the silence with, "They're scorched!" See, Mama always cooks her dumplings in her own special pot. This time she used one of mine because she was visiting. As we cooks know, it just isn't the same feel. Seldom do we gather together for chicken and dumplings when someone doesn't crack a joke about the day the never-go-wrong dumplings went terribly wrong.

SOUTHERN DRESSING AND GRAVY

Seems like at a lot of "meat and three" lunch places, Wednesday is dressing day. I guess that's because there might be leftover biscuits and cornbread by midweek. My grandmother Bramlett was always a frugal homemaker who didn't let a thing go to waste. This dressing is based on hers. Once you've accumulated enough leftover biscuits and cornbread—or made a batch of each—you can take to making your dressing. The wondrous melding of gravy and dressing is seamless.

Makes 10 to 12 servings

DRESSING

6 CUPS CRUMBLED CORNBREAD (SEE SOUTHERN SIMPLE)

2 CUPS CRUMBLED BISCUITS (SUCH AS MAW MAW'S BISCUITS, PAGE 44)

4 CUPS CHICKEN BROTH

1 CUP MILK

2 EGGS, BEATEN

1 CUP FINELY CHOPPED ONION

12 TABLESPOONS (1½ STICKS) BUTTER, 1 STICK MELTED AND ½ STICK COLD AND CUT INTO SMALL CUBES

1 TABLESPOON CHOPPED FRESH SAGE (OPTIONAL)

2 TEASPOONS SALT

1 TEASPOON FRESHLY GROUND BLACK PEPPER

GRAVY

4 TABLESPOONS (½ STICK) BUTTER

4 TABLESPOONS ALL-PURPOSE FLOUR

2 CUPS WHOLE MILK

1 CUP CHICKEN BROTH

SALT AND FRESHLY GROUND BLACK PEPPER

1. Preheat the oven to 375°F. Grease a 9 x 13-inch baking dish.

2. Make the dressing: In a large bowl, mix the cornbread, biscuits, chicken broth, milk, eggs, onion, 1 stick melted butter, sage, salt, and pepper. The consistency will be a little soupy. Pour the mixture into the prepared dish and dot with the ½ stick cold cubed butter. Bake until browned on top, about 45 minutes.

3. Meanwhile, make the gravy: Heat the butter in a small saucepan over low heat. Add the flour and cook, stirring constantly, until it comes together and starts

to foam, 1 to 2 minutes. Slowly whisk in the milk and continue to whisk until it becomes thick, about 5 minutes. Add the chicken broth and whisk to combine. Season with salt and pepper to taste.

4. Serve the dressing with the gravy.

SOUTHERN SIMPLE: For the cornbread in this recipe, I bake two packets of cornbread mix, such as Martha White, and crumble the cornbread when it's cooled.

SOUTHERN SIMPLE: The dressing can be assembled ahead of time and refrigerated. Add 15 minutes to the baking time if taking the casserole right from the refrigerator to the oven. The gravy can be made ahead of time and reheated; add a tablespoon or two of chicken broth to thin it if needed. I always try to err on the side of a bit too thin when making gravy, because it will thicken as it sits.

PEACH-ROASTED TURKEY

Most summers we try to get our whole passel of family together for a reunion. A roasted turkey is the easiest solution for a main course that will please everyone. The sunny taste of ripe peaches, along with fresh thyme and rosemary, gives this plump turkey a summer flavor so different from the fall flavors found in a traditional Thanksgiving bird.

Makes 8 servings

PEACH SAUCE

2 TABLESPOONS BUTTER

1 CUP CHOPPED YELLOW ONION

4 FRESH PEACHES, PEELED AND ROUGHLY CHOPPED, OR 2 CUPS CHOPPED FROZEN PEACH SLICES

2 TEASPOONS MUSTARD POWDER

½ CUP APPLE CIDER VINEGAR

1 CUP ORANGE JUICE

1 TABLESPOON SALT

TURKEY

ONE 12- TO 14-POUND WHOLE TURKEY

SALT AND FRESHLY GROUND BLACK PEPPER

2 PEACHES, PEELED AND QUARTERED, OR 1 CUP FROZEN PEACH SLICES

2 LEMONS, QUARTERED

10 THYME SPRIGS

10 ROSEMARY SPRIGS

1. Make the peach sauce: Melt the butter in a small saucepan over medium heat. Add the onion and cook until translucent, about 5 minutes. Add the peaches, mustard powder, vinegar, orange juice, and salt. Reduce the heat, cover, and simmer until the peaches are soft and cooked through, about 20 minutes. Puree the sauce in a food processor or blender until smooth.

2. For the turkey: Preheat the oven to 425°F.

3. Place the turkey in a roasting pan. Generously season the inside cavity of the turkey with salt and pepper. Stuff it with the peaches, lemon quarters, thyme, and rosemary. Tie the legs together with twine. Tuck the wings back and under the body to keep them from burning. You can also cover the wings with foil as they begin to brown, if needed.

(continued)

4. Fill a meat injector with peach sauce and inject the sauce into the turkey, making sure to hit every part to distribute the sauce evenly. The turkey will start to plump up, and you'll see the sauce ooze out a bit. Wipe it off, as it can burn. You'll have some leftover sauce, but use as much as you can to get that flavor in there. When all the parts are injected, generously season the outside of the turkey with salt and pepper. (Discard any remaining sauce.)

5. Roast the turkey until the skin is browned, about 45 minutes. Reduce the temperature to 350°F and continue to roast until a meat thermometer reads 165°F when inserted deep into the thigh (but away from the bone), 2 to 2½ hours (start checking at 2 hours). The juices in the thigh should run clear when pierced with a fork. Remove the turkey to a carving board and let it rest for 15 minutes before carving.

SOUTHERN SIMPLE: If there are any leftovers, try them in the Maple Monte Cristo Sandwich, page 210.

COUNTRY-FRIED STEAK AND MILK GRAVY

Some folks, like those from over in Texas, call this Chicken-Fried Steak. This was one of the first dinners I learned to cook. My mama taught me how to use a wooden spoon to scrape up all the browned bits in the pan after frying—and the secret of adding evaporated milk to make the richest gravy.

Makes 6 servings

½ CUP VEGETABLE OIL, PLUS MORE AS NEEDED

1½ CUPS ALL-PURPOSE FLOUR

1 TEASPOON SALT, PLUS MORE TO TASTE

½ TEASPOON FRESHLY GROUND BLACK PEPPER, PLUS MORE TO TASTE

1¾ CUPS MILK

SIX 4-OUNCE CUBE STEAKS OR TENDERIZED BEEF ROUND STEAKS (SEE SOUTHERN SIMPLE)

1½ CUPS EVAPORATED MILK

1. Heat the oil in a cast-iron skillet over medium heat. Combine 1¼ cups flour with the salt and pepper in a shallow bowl. Pour ½ cup of the milk into another shallow bowl. Season both sides of the steaks with salt and pepper. Dip the meat in the milk, then dredge it in the flour.

2. Add 2 or 3 steaks to the heated skillet and fry for 5 to 6 minutes on each side, until browned. Remove the steaks to a paper towel–lined plate to drain, then season them with salt. Repeat with the remaining steaks, adding oil to the pan as needed.

3. Remove all but about 3 tablespoons oil from the skillet. Add the remaining ¼ cup flour and stir with a wooden spoon, making sure to scrape the bits of crust from the bottom of the pan. Continue to stir until the flour is browned and bubbly. Slowly whisk in the evaporated milk. Whisk until there are no lumps and the gravy starts to thicken. Then add the remaining 1¼ cups milk. Reduce the heat to low and cook, stirring occasionally, for 10 minutes, or until the gravy is thickened to your preference. Season with salt and pepper to taste.

SOUTHERN SIMPLE: When at the meat counter, look for tenderized steaks labeled round steak, a cut from the round (or leg) of the cow, which lacks marbling. It's an inexpensive but relatively tough cut. If you do not find any that have already been "cubed" (tenderized), ask your butcher to give them a pass through his machine. The little ridges hold the coating well when the steaks are fried and give them just the right texture.

PORK TENDERLOIN WITH SLOW-COOKED APPLESAUCE

I grew up eating homemade applesauce that my grandmother Burrell made from the apple trees growing in her yard. When I became a mother, I started making it, too. While this applesauce is cooking down, the house fills with what I think heaven must smell like.

My brother-in-law Brian, preacher and father of four girls, taught me how to prepare these fast, flavorful pork tenderloins. It's his job at all family gatherings to make up his perfect pork tenderloins. He never disappoints! Children love this dish.

Makes 6 servings

APPLESAUCE

8 ASSORTED MEDIUM APPLES (SUCH AS FUJI, GALA, AND GOLDEN DELICIOUS),
    PEELED AND CUT INTO CHUNKS

1 CUP PACKED LIGHT BROWN SUGAR

1 CINNAMON STICK

GRATED ZEST AND JUICE OF 1 LEMON

¼ CUP APPLE CIDER

1 TEASPOON VANILLA EXTRACT

PORK TENDERLOIN

2 TABLESPOONS CHOPPED FRESH PARSLEY

2 TABLESPOONS CHOPPED FRESH THYME

2 TABLESPOONS CHOPPED FRESH ROSEMARY

GRATED ZEST AND JUICE OF 2 LEMONS

¼ CUP OLIVE OIL

2 TEASPOONS SALT

1 TEASPOON FRESHLY GROUND BLACK PEPPER

TWO 1-POUND PORK TENDERLOINS, FAT AND SILVER SKIN REMOVED

1. Make the applesauce. Dump all the ingredients into a slow cooker and cook on LOW for 7 to 8 hours, stirring occasionally. Use a potato masher to mash the applesauce to a thick, chunky consistency.

2. For the pork tenderloin: Preheat the oven to 375°F. Line a rimmed baking sheet with foil.

3. In a bowl, mix together the parsley, thyme, rosemary, lemon zest, lemon juice, olive oil, salt, and pepper. Rub the herb mixture all over the pork tenderloins. Place them in the prepared pan and roast until a meat thermometer reads 150°F, 20 to 25 minutes. Tent the pork with foil and let rest for 10 minutes before slicing.

4. Serve with warm slow-cooked applesauce.

SOUTHERN SIMPLE: This is a great dish to make when company is coming over because it makes the house smell so good. Just set the sauce to cooking in the morning; you can also coat the pork with the olive oil and herb mixture and keep it wrapped in the fridge. Then all you have to do is roast the pork and dinner is served.

SOUTHERN MOTHER: My daughter, Daisy, loves this applesauce. It will keep well in the refrigerator, or you can put it up proper in jars if you're up to a canning project. If your slow cooker can hold it, go on and double the batch—it's always nice to have on hand for playdates.

Grandmother Burrell's Mexican Cornbread

I can see my grandmother in my mind's eye with her apron tied up high on her waist, a dishrag tucked in the strings, and all sorts of pots on the stove. She would spend all day in the kitchen if she could. She just loved being right there in the middle of everything, jokes and giggles a-flowing! When she baked this spicy cornbread, she'd make batch after batch and me and my sweet cousins Shaina and Hailey would not let a batch sit around for long. Whatever muffins were left she would wrap in a dish towel and send home with us.

This cornbread is good served with chili, of course, but it's wonderful just the way she'd give it to me: sliced with a little pat of butter tucked inside. I love spending all day in the kitchen cooking for the ones I love, just like my sweet Grams. I miss her!

Makes 4 servings

1½ CUPS SELF-RISING CORNMEAL

3 EGGS

ONE 14.75-OUNCE CAN CREAM-STYLE CORN

1 CUP GRATED SHARP CHEDDAR CHEESE

1 RED BELL PEPPER, FINELY DICED

2 JALAPEÑOS, SEEDED AND MINCED

½ CUP CANOLA OIL

1. Preheat the oven to 425°F. Place a 9-inch cast-iron skillet in the oven to heat up—you want the cast iron hot before you pour the batter in. This makes for a really good cornbread.

2. Mix all the ingredients together in a bowl. Pour it into the hot skillet and place it in the oven. Bake until the cornbread is golden brown and a toothpick inserted in the center comes out clean, about 20–25 minutes.

> **SOUTHERN SIMPLE:** This cornbread bakes up well as muffins, too. Just make sure you coat the tins well with cooking spray to ensure that they don't stick.

> **SOUTHERN SIMPLE:** Try this cornbread with the Manly Man Brunswick Stew (page 16) for a dinner sure to please the man in your life.
> For a quick lunch, crumble this cornbread over a bowl of black-eyed peas.

> **SOUTHERN MOTHER:** If your kids haven't developed a real taste for hot flavors yet, trade the jalapeños for 2 tablespoons finely chopped green bell pepper.

HUSH PUPPIES

My grandfather Papa Burrell loved to fish. He'd make me and my little sister and cousins squeal as he sat outside cleaning fish right before a fish fry. We would prance and skip around, waiting for a chance to grab one of those deep-fried delights called hush puppies. He'd always hand them over to us and say, "Now hush, you puppies!"

Makes 18 hush puppies

VEGETABLE OIL FOR DEEP-FRYING

½ CUP ALL-PURPOSE FLOUR

½ CUP YELLOW CORNMEAL

½ TEASPOON SALT, PLUS MORE FOR SEASONING

½ TEASPOON FRESHLY GROUND BLACK PEPPER

¼ TEASPOON BAKING SODA

1 LARGE EGG

½ CUP BUTTERMILK

¼ CUP MINCED ONION

¼ CUP SEEDED AND MINCED JALAPEÑOS

1. Pour enough oil into a large cast-iron skillet to come up halfway. Place the skillet over medium heat and heat the oil to 375°F.

2. Combine the flour, cornmeal, and ½ teaspoon each salt and pepper in a large bowl. Make a well in the center of the mixture.

3. Whisk together the egg and buttermilk in a small bowl. Pour the buttermilk mixture into the well in the dry ingredients. Mix with a wooden spoon until just moistened. Stir in the onion and the jalapeños. For the lightest hush puppies, let the batter sit for 2 minutes or so before you fry.

4. Working in batches to make sure there's plenty of room to cook, drop the batter by the tablespoon into the hot oil and fry until golden brown, about 3 minutes on each side. Drain the hush puppies on paper towels and season them with salt. Serve immediately.

SOUTHERN SIMPLE: This batter may seem a little on the wet side, but trust me—that's what makes these fry up so nice and so light. I sure wouldn't give these to the dogs.

SOUTHERN SIMPLE: These are even good for a passed-around party snack when you aren't having a fish fry. Try them with the Hot Ranch Dip that goes with the onion rings on page 114.

Maw Maw's Biscuits

Daisy calls my mother Maw Maw. Since my mother taught me how to make these biscuits, I call them Maw Maw's Biscuits.

To me, a biscuit is a magical thing. How can three simple ingredients come together to create such joy? Once you get the hang and feel of making biscuits, you can turn them out in no time flat. A couple of things to remember when you're making biscuits: don't work the dough too much and use a sharp cutter so the edges rise nicely. I know people who just use a juice glass to cut their biscuits. Use whatever you've got, but a nice cutter will make you a prizewinning biscuit.

Makes 8 biscuits

2 CUPS SELF-RISING FLOUR, SIFTED

4 TABLESPOONS BUTTER, COLD AND CUT INTO CUBES, AND AN ADDITIONAL 2 TABLESPOONS MELTED

¾ CUP COLD MILK

1. Preheat the oven to 450°F. Grease a 9-inch cast-iron skillet.

2. Use your hands or a pastry blender to mix the flour and 4 tablespoons cold butter in a bowl until it feels crumbly. Add the milk and mix well, but don't overwork the dough. Knead the dough just a couple of times, then on a lightly floured surface roll it out to a ½-inch thickness. Cut the dough into biscuits using a 3-inch round cutter. Knead the leftover scraps of dough and roll and cut again so that you get a total of 8 biscuits.

3. Place the biscuits in the prepared skillet. It will be snug, and they will be touching. Bake for 12 minutes. Generously brush the 2 tablespoons melted butter on top of the biscuits and return them to the oven until golden brown, about 3 more minutes.

SOUTHERN SIMPLE: We often roll and cut out the biscuits 15 to 30 minutes before guests arrive, cover them uncooked in the refrigerator, then bake them just in time to have hot biscuits without the mess. But don't leave them in the refrigerator longer than 30 minutes.

(continued)

SOUTHERN SIMPLE: Usually there aren't any biscuits left, but when there are I add them to a bag I keep in the freezer and then use them later for making Southern Dressing and Gravy (page 32).

If you've never had sorghum and butter on a warm biscuit, then, my friend, you've missed one of life's simple pleasures. Sorghum cane is processed into syrup in a fashion similar to processing sugar cane. The flavor is a little milder than molasses and a bit less sweet than honey.

SOUTHERN MOTHER: I grew up thinking everybody had homemade biscuits for supper every night. I'm glad my mama made us feel that way. She most likely learned that from *her* grandmother. My great-grandmother Grandma Burrell was mother to six kids. She was an angel of a lady and a pro at making biscuits. She probably could have made them in her sleep. She used to cook thirty biscuits every morning before her boys went to work out in the fields! She wanted their tummies to be full. A tummy full of biscuits can yield a whole crop of good vittles! She would also cook up that many biscuits at night. My great-aunt Maxine fondly remembers standing by her mama while she would make a little well of flour in her biscuit bowl and add the milk and lard. She would then pinch off pieces of dough, slap them on a pan, and give them a little pat with the back of her fingers. She certainly had a system. How else could one woman make five dozen biscuits a day!

If you ever find yourself down in my neck of the woods around October, take a field trip to the Museum of Appalachia, where they have a working cane mill and a wonderful lineup of bluegrass, old-time, and Americana music at their annual Fall Homecoming Festival.

GRANNY BECK'S APPLE BUTTER

This recipe came by way of my sister-in-law Jade, who comes from a long line of incredibly sweet and hilariously entertaining women. When you get them all together, a party spontaneously combusts! Her Granny Beck has made this apple butter for as long as Jade can remember. If folks are at her table—whether for breakfast, lunch, or dinner—there's a little crock of this sweet apple spread on the table. It's as if it's just waiting to hop on a biscuit! Jade and my brother, Josh, have a little girl of their own. In my family, we seem to have a knack for making adorable baby girls, if I do say so myself!

Makes about 8 cups

6 POUNDS APPLES (ABOUT 16 MEDIUM), WASHED, UNPEELED, QUARTERED, AND CORED

1 CUP APPLE CIDER

1 CUP WATER

5 CUPS SUGAR

1 TABLESPOON GROUND CINNAMON

1 TEASPOON GROUND CLOVES

½ TEASPOON GROUND ALLSPICE

1. Place the apples in a large pot with the cider and water and place over low heat. Let the apples simmer uncovered until they begin to break down and soften, about 30 minutes. Use a potato masher to help break them down as they cook. Pass the apples through a coarse sieve. Discard the solids.

2. Pour the apple mixture back into the pot and mix in the sugar, cinnamon, cloves, and allspice. Let the mixture simmer uncovered over low heat, stirring frequently, until it turns a deep caramel color, about 2 hours. Cooking time may vary depending on the variety of apples you use. Store apple butter in the refrigerator for up to two weeks.

SOUTHERN SIMPLE: Make a batch of this to serve with Maw Maw's Biscuits (page 44). I also love this on a piece of leftover cornbread.

SOUTHERN SIMPLE: Apple butter is wonderful spread on a grilled pork chop or turkey tenderloin, too . . .
    Or try the apple butter on a sharp Cheddar grilled cheese or as an addition to the Maple Monte Cristo Sandwich (page 210).

SOUTHERN MOTHER: Joshua and Jade did the sweetest thing at their wedding. Each guest received a little Mason jar of Granny Beck's Apple Butter with this recipe attached. So cute and creative!

VINEGAR PECAN PIE

The name vinegar pie may be off-putting to some folks. Traditionally, vinegar was added to sweet pies for a touch of acid when lemons or apples were not available. Just a few dashes of vinegar add a tang to balance the sweet things out. I love pecans, but so many pecan pie recipes are just too sweet for me, like the ones with all that corn syrup. This is just the type of pie I love—not too sweet, with a pecan crunch.

Makes one 9-inch pie

6 TABLESPOONS (¾ STICK) MARGARINE

1 CUP SUGAR

2 EGGS

3½ TEASPOONS DISTILLED WHITE VINEGAR

1 TEASPOON VANILLA EXTRACT

2 TEASPOONS SELF-RISING FLOUR

½ CUP CHOPPED PECANS

ONE 9-INCH STORE-BOUGHT PIE SHELL

1. Preheat the oven to 350°F.

2. Melt the margarine in a small saucepan over low heat. Whisk together the sugar, eggs, vinegar, vanilla, flour, and pecans in a large bowl. Slowly pour in the melted margarine, a little at a time, and mix until well incorporated.

3. Pour the batter into the pie shell and bake until golden brown and the center does not jiggle when shaken lightly, about 30 minutes. Let the pie cool for 15 minutes before serving.

SOUTHERN SIMPLE: I try to keep prepared pie shells in the freezer. This pie is always a go-to for me because I usually have all the ingredients on hand, plus it's a favorite of my bandmate Karen's.

It's best to store pecans and other nuts in the freezer.

Fresh Glazed Apple Cake

A precious little lady named Mrs. Coffee taught my daddy in school. By the time I was coming up she had slowed her pace and taught only as a substitute teacher. She was a member of our church and was especially known for her deliciously moist apple cake. I liked having a teacher who had known my daddy when he was in school. Daddy has always been curious and interested in learning. He even took up pottery at the age of sixty-eight. When I bake this cake, I like to serve it on the beautiful ceramic cake stand my daddy made for me, and when I drizzle the apple glaze over the cake I think about sweet little Mrs. Coffee and how important it is to keep on learning.

Makes 1 Bundt cake

CAKE

1¼ CUPS CANOLA OIL

2 CUPS SUGAR

3 EGGS, AT ROOM TEMPERATURE

2 TEASPOONS VANILLA EXTRACT

3 CUPS ALL-PURPOSE FLOUR

1 TEASPOON BAKING SODA

1 TEASPOON SALT

1 TEASPOON GROUND CINNAMON

4 CUPS PEELED AND DICED ASSORTED
    APPLES

1 CUP FINELY CHOPPED PECANS
    (OPTIONAL)

GLAZE

¾ CUP SUGAR

½ CUP EVAPORATED MILK

8 TABLESPOONS (1 STICK) SALTED BUTTER

1. Make the cake: Preheat the oven to 325°F. Grease and lightly flour a Bundt pan.

2. Using an electric mixer, cream the oil and sugar in a large bowl. Add the eggs and vanilla and mix well. Sift in the flour, baking soda, salt, and cinnamon. Mix until well incorporated. The batter will be on the thick side. Add the apples and pecans to the bowl and mix well.

(continued)

3. Pour the batter into the Bundt pan and bake until a toothpick inserted in the center of the cake comes out clean, about 1 hour 10 minutes.

4. Meanwhile, make the glaze: Combine the sugar, evaporated milk, and butter in a small saucepan and set over medium heat. Cook, stirring, for 3 minutes. Keep warm.

5. When the cake is done, leave it in the pan. Poke holes all over the cake with a skewer or toothpick. Pour three-quarters of the glaze on top of the cake while it's in the pan and still hot. The holes will help soak up the glaze. Let it rest for 30 minutes. Invert the cake onto a cake plate and pour the remaining glaze on top. (If needed, heat the glaze slightly over low heat to bring it to a nice consistency for pouring.)

SOUTHERN MOTHER: My little one loves to take a bamboo skewer and poke about a million holes in this cake when it comes out of the oven. Then she'll help pour some of the glaze over the cake and watch it seep down into the holes. Oh, it's the moistest cake!

SOUTHERN MOTHER: I combined a couple of recipes to come up with this one. I use Mrs. Coffee's glaze and my grandmother's cake!

GRAM'S SHEET CAKE

This is a special sheet cake. What makes it so special? Why, it can be turned into so many things! My grandmother Burrell always had one or two of these sheet cakes in the deep freeze. Forgotten birthday? No problem: just take it out and top it with frosting and candles. Drop-in company? Just let it thaw during dinner and serve with sweetened whipped cream and fresh fruit. School bake sale? Ice it in school colors and cut it into squares.

If I know these are headed right to the freezer, I bake the cakes in disposable bakeware.

Makes one 9 x 13-inch sheet cake

CAKE

3 CUPS ALL-PURPOSE FLOUR

⅔ CUP SELF-RISING FLOUR

¼ TEASPOON SALT

3 CUPS SUGAR

1½ CUPS VEGETABLE SHORTENING

6 EGGS, AT ROOM TEMPERATURE

1½ CUPS MILK

2 TEASPOONS ALMOND EXTRACT

1. Make the cake: Preheat the oven to 350°F. Grease and lightly flour a 9 x 13-inch sheet cake pan.

2. Sift the flours and salt together into a medium bowl. Using an electric mixer, cream the sugar and shortening in a large bowl until very light and fluffy. Beat in the eggs one at a time, mixing after each addition. Add the flour mixture and milk alternately to the creamed mixture, beginning and ending with the flour, mixing just until incorporated after each addition. Add the almond extract.

3. Pour the batter into the cake pan and spread it out evenly. Bake until a toothpick inserted in the center comes out clean, 40 to 50 minutes. Let the cake cool in the pan for 5 to 10 minutes.

SOUTHERN SIMPLE: These cakes keep well in the freezer. Make sure they're wrapped well so they don't take on any odd flavor from the freezer.

SOUTHERN MOTHER: This is a good recipe to make with kids. It's straightforward, and they love getting to top it with whatever they choose when it's ready to serve. Ice cream and chocolate chips with colored sprinkles goes over big at our house.

Grandmother's Coconut Pudding

This is like bread pudding. Well, like bread pudding but with cake and topped with meringue! Slices of pound cake soak up the sweet coconut custard, then the pudding is blanketed in fluffy meringue.

Makes one 9 x 13-inch cake

ONE 12-OUNCE STORE-BOUGHT POUND CAKE, CUT INTO 1-INCH-THICK SLICES

½ CUP WHOLE MILK

2¼ CUPS (18 OUNCES) EVAPORATED MILK

1½ CUPS PLUS 1 TABLESPOON SUGAR

6 TABLESPOONS (¾ STICK) BUTTER

½ CUP ALL-PURPOSE FLOUR

4 EGGS, AT ROOM TEMPERATURE, SEPARATED

2 CUPS SWEETENED SHREDDED COCONUT

2 TEASPOONS VANILLA EXTRACT

1. Preheat the oven to 350°F.

2. Arrange one layer of cake slices on the bottom of a 9 x 13-inch baking dish, cutting slices to fit.

3. Combine the milk, evaporated milk, 1½ cups of the sugar, the flour, and butter in a medium saucepan. Set over low heat and whisk until the sugar and flour dissolve and the butter melts. Slowly whisk in the egg yolks and cook, whisking constantly, until the mixture starts to thicken, 4 to 6 minutes. Add the coconut and 1 teaspoon of the vanilla. Continue to whisk and cook for 6 to 8 minutes, until it becomes thick.

4. Pour the pudding evenly over the cake slices in the baking dish.

5. Using an electric mixer, beat the egg whites in a large bowl until bubbly and foamy. Add the remaining 1 tablespoon sugar and the remaining 1 teaspoon vanilla and beat until soft peaks form. Spread the meringue over the pudding mixture and bake until golden brown, 20 to 25 minutes. Let cool in the pan for 10 to 15 minutes before serving. Serve immediately or refrigerate, covered, for 1 day.

(continued)

SOUTHERN SIMPLE: When beating egg whites, make sure not a speck of yolk gets in and that your bowl and beaters are squeaky clean, without a trace of fat or buttery fingerprints, so your whites will whip up to their highest height.

SOUTHERN SIMPLE: Look for sweetened shredded coconut in the grocer's freezer. It has a fresher taste than the bags in the baking aisle.

SOUTHERN MOTHER: A can of evaporated milk shows up in many, many old Southern recipes. Obviously convenience is one reason, since having shelf-stable milk in the pantry is always handy, and many of these recipes have come from Depression-era rural areas and before many homes had electricity to run a refrigerator. Evaporated milk is also richer than whole milk and can bake longer and at a higher temperature without separating.

CHRISTMAS COFFEE PUNCH

My mother makes a tremendous batch of this festive drink and sets it up in a punch bowl right inside the front door at Christmastime. A big punch bowl with little cups and candy canes for garnish is a treat for grown folks during the holiday hustle and bustle.

Makes 36 cups

1 CUP INSTANT COFFEE GRANULES

2 CUPS SUGAR

ONE 16-OUNCE CAN HERSHEY'S CHOCOLATE SYRUP

1 TABLESPOON VANILLA EXTRACT

1 GALLON WHOLE MILK

6 QUARTS VANILLA ICE CREAM

CANDY CANES, FOR GARNISH

1. Combine the instant coffee and 3 quarts water in a large pot and heat over medium-high heat until the coffee dissolves. Add the sugar, chocolate syrup, and vanilla. Stir until the sugar is dissolved.

2. Refrigerate the mixture until completely chilled. Place it in the freezer for 30 minutes or longer before serving. You want it extra cold and a little icy.

3. When you're ready to serve the punch, pour the mixture into a large punch bowl. Stir in the milk and scoop in the ice cream. If your punch bowl isn't big enough, just keep refilling it as needed—this makes a big batch! Serve with candy canes hooked on the rim of each cup.

SOUTHERN SIMPLE: It's great to make the coffee base several days ahead of when you plan to serve it, since the mixture has to chill before serving. Freeze the base for several days, thaw until slushy, and stir in the milk and ice cream.

SOUTHERN SIMPLE: You can change up the flavors of this punch. Try it with dulce de leche–flavored ice cream and a sprinkle of cinnamon for a Feliz Navidad fiesta.

CHAPTER 2

Friends

I am surely blessed by good friends in my life. I love cooking for them almost as much as I love cooking with them. Back in grade school, my friend Pam Baker and I would take turns spending the night at each other's homes. Well, there's nothing as silly or determined as a couple of grade-school girls. One night when Pam was at my house for a sleepover, we got up the notion to make a pink meringue pie. We pored over a recipe from a new kids' cookbook I had recently gotten and just had to break in. We assembled all the ingredients. Things were going pretty well until it was time to make the meringue. Mama allowed us to use the electric hand-mixer, a decision she soon regretted. Grade school girls + electric mixer—you probably know where this is going. Things took a bad turn when it quickly became evident that I didn't yet understand the finer points of running an electric hand-mixer. I raised the beaters out of the bowl of fluffy pink meringue with that thing running full speed. You can imagine the catastrophe that ensued. We had slung pink meringue from floor to ceiling and everywhere in between. Mama was cleaning our disaster out from under her cabinets for weeks. It was amazing the places she found it.

By high school I had perfected the back-of-the-bag chocolate chip cookie recipe and made cookies for my friends for any and all occasions. I had also begun to take more and more interest in cooking.

One semester in college my friend Heather Meeks and I were roomies. We loved to cook. On Valentine's Day we decided we would make a special breakfast for some fellows. That would have been all fine and dandy, but we got the bright idea to color everything red. I mean everything: the grits, the muffins, and even the eggs. The breakfast would have tasted great if the fellows had been blindfolded. What were we thinking? Those red eggs just took things too far!

I do love my bandmates. We've lived through a lot of life together. We're like family, and when the band first came together, we would meet at my house a lot because I was centrally located between everybody. Karen, Jimi, and Phillip would come over and we would brainstorm ideas like band names or musical direction, and we'd work up songs.

And I would always cook. A good rehearsal cannot happen without some good sustenance! I like to try out new recipes on them. They were actually my willing guinea pigs for some of the recipes in this book.

To this day, as busy as life is, I love to have a birthday goody for each of them and the folks in the band crew on their special day.

SIMPLY SOUTHERN BOILED PEANUTS

If there's a big game, big race, big road trip, or big party on my calendar and I know I'm going to hit the ground running, I mark the day before on my calendar as "Boiled Peanut Day." Then when that afternoon rolls around, I put the peanuts on to cook in super-salty water. I go about my business, but check on them every now and then and give them a stir. If the water has gotten down to where the peanuts are popping above the water, I'll top off the water a little. By the next morning, the peanuts are done. I let them cool in the pot, then refrigerate the pot and all. The day of the big event I can keep them warm and ready to serve in a slow cooker. Planning ahead is a whole lot more fun than having folks sitting around and taking the lid off your peanut pot, asking when they're going to be ready!

Makes 8 servings

2 POUNDS SHELL-ON RAW PEANUTS
¾ CUP KOSHER SALT

Rinse the peanuts with water. Place the peanuts and the salt in a 6-quart slow cooker. Cover with water. Cover and cook on HIGH for 18 hours, stirring occasionally to disperse the salt. Make sure the peanuts are always submerged during the cooking process. You will need to add a little water now and then as the peanuts are cooking.

SOUTHERN SKINNY: Peanuts pack in 7 grams of protein per ounce.

SOUTHERN SIMPLE: If you have spicy food fans coming, you can do as they do in truck stops: serve one batch of Louisiana-spiced and one batch of regular salted. To make Louisiana-style boiled peanuts, replace the salt with a seasoning blend like Zatarain's Creole Seasoning or Tony Chachere's Creole Seasoning.

GEORGIA PEACH SALSA

I love the girly names of peach varieties, such as Elegant Lady, Spring Lady, White Lady, and Summer Lady. There's even one variety named Rich Lady. When these "ladies" are in season, around the month of July, I make this salsa.

You need perfectly ripe peaches to make this salsa. Ripe peaches will smell pleasingly sweet and won't have "green shoulders." Remember that Crimson Blush is just the variety—not a sign of ripeness. Also, handle them gingerly, because even firm fruit will show bruises later if knocked around. If your peaches are a bit underripe, store them in a cool room, stem side down, for a couple of days. When you start to notice that sweet peachy smell, they're ready to go into this salsa and get dressed up with a little frilly cilantro and a bright squeeze of lime.

Makes 4 cups

4 PEACHES, PEELED, PITTED, AND CUT INTO SMALL DICE

½ CUP FINELY DICED RED BELL PEPPER

¼ CUP MINCED RED ONION

1 JALAPEÑO, SEEDED AND MINCED

3 TABLESPOONS CHOPPED FRESH CILANTRO

JUICE OF 1 LIME

SALT AND FRESHLY GROUND BLACK PEPPER TO TASTE

Combine all the ingredients in a bowl and mix well. Let the salsa sit for 30 minutes to let the flavors blend. Serve immediately or refrigerate until ready to serve.

SOUTHERN SIMPLE: For an easy lunch or summer dinner, I serve the salsa with my Southwest Tortilla Roll-Ups (page 126).

SOUTHERN SKINNY: Serve this salsa with some baked tortilla chips for a fresh midday snack, or use it as a flavorful topping for a piece of grilled fish.

My great friend, photographer, and fellow Georgian Becky Fluke always brings me a box of peaches from South Georgia when she goes home to visit family in the summer. A box of sweet Georgia peaches is the perfect way to celebrate a sweet friendship.

Cucumber and Tomato Salad

As much as I love sweets, I love sour flavors, too. I was one of the kids who would opt for a big dill pickle at the picture show or ball field concession stand. This easy-to-prepare, lightly pickled salad has the right amount of sweet and sour for me.

Makes 8 servings

1 CUP DISTILLED WHITE VINEGAR

¾ CUP SUGAR

3 CUCUMBERS, HALVED LENGTHWISE, SEEDED, AND CUT CROSSWISE INTO HALF-MOONS

1 MEDIUM SWEET ONION, THINLY SLICED

4 TOMATOES, CUT INTO MEDIUM DICE

2 TEASPOONS CHOPPED FRESH DILL

¼ TEASPOON SALT

1. Combine the vinegar, sugar, and ½ cup water in a small saucepan and bring to a boil over medium heat, stirring until the sugar dissolves. Remove from the heat and cool.

2. Place the cucumbers, onion, and tomatoes in a large glass bowl. Pour the liquid over the vegetables and add the dill and salt. Gently toss. Refrigerate for at least 6 hours or up to 3 days.

COLLARD GREEN GRILLED CHEESE

Musicians sometimes keep odd hours. When I get home late, grilled cheese sandwiches are always what I crave. A bag of washed-and-ready collard greens from the grocer helps these come together with no fuss. A slice of tomato and an English muffin make for a satisfying meal when this sandwich comes out of the skillet. My little buddy, songstress Kellie Pickler, is a vegetarian, and she absolutely loved this sandwich when I served it to her along with a bowl of Apple-Tomato Soup (page 149).

Makes 4 sandwiches

1 POUND COLLARD GREENS, WASHED, STEMS AND CENTER RIB REMOVED, AND CHOPPED, OR ONE 16-OUNCE BAG COLLARD GREENS

2 TABLESPOONS BUTTER, PLUS MORE FOR GRILLING

2 TABLESPOONS OLIVE OIL

3 GARLIC CLOVES, MINCED

1 TABLESPOON RED PEPPER FLAKES

SALT AND FRESHLY GROUND BLACK PEPPER

JUICE OF 1 LEMON

4 ENGLISH MUFFINS, SPLIT APART

8 SLICES HAVARTI CHEESE

1 GREEN TOMATO, SLICED

1. Cook the collards in a large pot of boiling water until tender, about 30 minutes. Drain in a colander and press out the excess liquid with the back of a wooden spoon, or let them cool and squeeze out the liquid with your hands.

2. Heat the 2 tablespoons butter and the olive oil in a large skillet over medium heat until the foam subsides. Stir in the garlic, pepper flakes, and collards. Season with salt and black pepper to taste. Cook, stirring, for about 5 minutes to evaporate the liquid. Add the lemon juice and toss well.

3. Generously butter the outside of each muffin half, top and bottom.

4. Heat a large skillet over low heat and toast the cut sides of the muffins until lightly browned. To build the sandwich, place a piece of cheese on the top and bottom of each muffin. Place one slice of tomato on each bottom. Fill each sandwich with collard greens on top of the tomato. Place a muffin top on each sandwich. (The layers from top to bottom should be: bread, cheese, collard greens, tomato, cheese, bread.)

5. Place the sandwiches in the pan to toast for about 4 minutes on each side, until golden brown and toasted and the cheese is nicely melted.

SOUTHERN SIMPLE: Look for bags of washed, stemmed, and torn collard greens in the produce section.

SOUTHERN SIMPLE: This is a super way to use up just about any leftover vegetables. Make sure you really squeeze out any excess liquid to ensure that the sandwiches grill up crisp.

CHICKEN AND HERB WHITE PIZZA

One of the favorite features of my home is the "greenhouse" bay window in the kitchen. It was my husband Schlappy's brilliant idea, and I kiss him on the mouth for it just about every day! It makes me so happy, and I keep little pots of herbs growing there. It's nice to have that bit of flavor on hand. With a few snips I have fresh basil, oregano, and parsley to season the chicken for this creamy pizza. I'll add the herbs to the chicken right before I top the pizza; this keeps the flavors bright and the herbs from overcooking and losing their pop.

Makes one 12-inch pizza

1 CUP WHOLE MILK

3 GARLIC CLOVES, MINCED

2 TABLESPOONS BUTTER

2 TABLESPOONS ALL-PURPOSE FLOUR

¼ TEASPOON SALT

¼ TEASPOON CAYENNE PEPPER

¼ TEASPOON FRESHLY GROUND BLACK PEPPER

4 OUNCES FONTINA CHEESE, CUBED

2 TABLESPOONS OLIVE OIL

2 BONELESS, SKINLESS CHICKEN BREAST HALVES, CUT INTO SMALL PIECES

1 TEASPOON CHOPPED FRESH BASIL

1 TEASPOON CHOPPED FRESH OREGANO

1 TEASPOON CHOPPED FRESH CHIVES

1 TEASPOON CHOPPED FRESH PARSLEY

YELLOW CORNMEAL FOR DUSTING

1 BALL STORE-BOUGHT PIZZA DOUGH, ROLLED OUT TO A 12-INCH CIRCLE

½ CUP QUARTERED CHERRY TOMATOES

¾ CUP SHREDDED MOZZARELLA CHEESE

1. Preheat the oven to 500°F.

2. Gently heat the milk in a small saucepan over low heat, just until barely simmering. Remove from the heat, add the garlic, and let it infuse the milk for 5 to 10 minutes.

3. Melt the butter in a separate saucepan. When the foam subsides, add the flour and whisk until smooth. Keep whisking for 1 to 2 minutes; do not allow the flour to color. Gradually add the warm milk and garlic, whisking to combine. Add the salt

and cayenne and increase the heat to medium. Cook the mixture, whisking constantly, until the sauce comes to a boil and is thickened, about 10 minutes. Reduce the heat, add the fontina, and whisk until it melts. Transfer the cheese sauce to a small bowl and cool slightly, placing a piece of plastic wrap directly on the surface.

4. Heat the olive oil in a large skillet over medium-high heat. Add the chicken and cook until cooked through, about 5 minutes. Season with salt and pepper to taste. Add all the herbs and stir. Remove from the heat.

5. Sprinkle some of the cornmeal on a baking sheet. Place the rolled-out pizza dough on the baking sheet and shape it as desired.

6. Spread the cheese sauce over the dough, leaving a 1-inch border of the crust free of sauce. Top the pizza with the chicken-herb mixture, tomatoes, and mozzarella. Bake until the crust is golden brown and crispy, 7 to 10 minutes. Cut the pizza into 8 wedges and serve immediately.

SOUTHERN SIMPLE: You can visit your local pizza shop and purchase premade pizza dough from them (it will also work for the Sweet Orange Rolls on page 178). Leave it to the experts to make the dough . . . then all you have to worry about are the toppings.

SOUTHERN MOTHER: Pick up an extra ball of pizza dough for the kids to play with while you create a pizza masterpiece for the grown-ups. My Daisy can make quite the creation with a ball of dough! Speaking of my little chef, when I was pregnant with her, this particular pizza was one of my cravings.

THREE-ALARM ENCHILADAS

My dear friend Sheila brought our family a dish of these spicy chicken enchiladas soon after Daisy was born. It was such a thoughtful gesture, particularly after that last trimester. I was so ready to get back to some spicy foods!

Makes 12 enchiladas

TWO 10.75-OUNCE CANS CONDENSED CREAM OF CHICKEN SOUP

½ CUP MILK

16 OUNCES (ABOUT 2 CUPS) SOUR CREAM

¼ CUP DICED ONION

3 JALAPEÑOS, SEEDED AND FINELY DICED

2 TABLESPOONS HOT SAUCE

2 CUPS COOKED SHREDDED CHICKEN

2 CUPS GRATED MONTEREY JACK CHEESE

CANOLA OIL, FOR FRYING

TWELVE 6-INCH CORN TORTILLAS

2 TABLESPOONS CHOPPED FRESH CILANTRO

LIME WEDGES, FOR GARNISH

MEDIUM OR HOT SALSA, FOR SERVING

1. Preheat the oven to 350°F.

2. Combine the soup, milk, sour cream, onion, jalapeños, and hot sauce in a bowl. Spread ½ cup of the mixture over the bottom of a 9 x 13-inch baking dish. Add the chicken and 1½ cups of the Jack cheese to the remaining soup mixture.

3. Pour enough oil into a medium skillet to come up ¼ inch. Heat the oil over medium heat until it shimmers. Fry the tortillas for 10 seconds per side. Stack them between paper towels as they're done.

4. Fill each tortilla with ⅓ cup of the chicken mixture. Roll and place in the baking dish, seam side down. Spread the remaining soup mixture evenly over the tortillas. Sprinkle with the remaining cheese.

5. Bake until the cheese melts and bubbles, about 35 minutes. Top with the cilantro and garnish with fresh lime wedges. Serve with salsa for more spice.

SOUTHERN SIMPLE: Pick up a rotisserie chicken at the market to get a head start on this casserole.

I dropped out of kindergarten. After the first few weeks of school, the teachers lined us up single file for a fire drill. When the alarm sounded and they marched us out, it scared me so badly! I cried and cried so hard they had to call my mother. She sent Daddy to pick me up. He told me in the car on the way home, "Baby, now, next year when you start first grade, you can't just drop out. Okay, baby doll?"

ROSEMARY PORK CHOPS

It's funny how family sayings get picked up by friends. When I was around ten and my sister was about five, we were acting up at the dinner table. My daddy had worked a long hard day, and when he couldn't take another minute of our shenanigans, he pushed his chair back, folded his dinner napkin, and left the table. Totally unaffected by his frustration, my innocent little sister immediately piped up: "Can I have Daddy's pork chop?" I've often told friends that funny tale over the years. Now when I serve pork chops and someone wants seconds they'll chime in, "Can I have Daddy's pork chop?"

Makes 4 servings

½ CUP PLUS 2 TABLESPOONS OLIVE OIL

⅓ CUP RED WINE VINEGAR

4 ROSEMARY SPRIGS, PLUS 1 TABLESPOON MINCED FRESH ROSEMARY

3 GARLIC CLOVES, SMASHED AND ROUGHLY CHOPPED

1 TABLESPOON PACKED LIGHT BROWN SUGAR

FOUR ½-INCH-THICK BONELESS PORK CHOPS

SALT AND FRESHLY GROUND BLACK PEPPER

ALL-PURPOSE FLOUR, FOR DREDGING

1. Combine ½ cup of the olive oil, the vinegar, rosemary sprigs, garlic, and brown sugar in a large zip-top bag. Add the pork chops to the marinade and seal. Massage the chops in the bag to coat them well. Refrigerate for at least 2 hours to marinate.

2. Remove the pork chops from the marinade and pat them dry. (Discard the marinade.) Let the pork chops come to room temperature for 15 minutes. Season with salt and pepper on both sides, then dredge them in flour.

3. Heat the remaining 2 tablespoons olive oil in a large skillet over medium heat. Add the pork and panfry until they're cooked through, 4 to 6 minutes per side. Sprinkle the remaining rosemary on top of the chops at the very end for more flavor.

SOUTHERN SIMPLE: If you're in a time or ingredient pinch, replace the rosemary and garlic in the marinade with 1 tablespoon of pesto.

Speaking of my sis, she's also my best girlfriend. With all the miles between us, we stay tightly connected. She's Wonder Woman. She has four gorgeous girls, runs her own business—she's a music therapist—and is a preacher's wife! She had kiddos first, so I learned so much from her about being a working mom. We have too much fun together and are always up for an adventure, be it in the big city of New York, New York, or the tiny town of Hollywood, Georgia. She is incredibly supportive of me and keeps me grounded.

CHEDDAR BACON BISCUITS

I adore an occasional breakfast for supper at night. It's just fun and kooky to have biscuits and scrambled eggs for dinner, especially when you have a house full of company and everyone has been out playing all day. I like for everybody to get in their flannels early, then lend a hand in the kitchen. Surely somebody in the crowd can scramble eggs, and I know I can get my hubby cooking up the bacon, and the kiddos can set the table just the way they want it. These savory cheese biscuits are the centerpiece of an easy, engaging meal to feed a whole house party.

Makes 6 biscuits

8 SLICES THICK-CUT BACON, FINELY CHOPPED

1 CUP FINELY CHOPPED ONION

2 CUPS ALL-PURPOSE FLOUR

1 TABLESPOON BAKING POWDER

1 TEASPOON SALT

1 TEASPOON PAPRIKA

1 CUP BUTTERMILK

8 TABLESPOONS (1 STICK) BUTTER, MELTED

1 CUP SHREDDED CHEDDAR CHEESE

1. Preheat the oven to 425°F.

2. Cook the bacon in a large skillet over medium heat, stirring occasionally, until crispy, 5 to 7 minutes. Drain the bacon on paper towels. Pour off (and reserve) all but 1 tablespoon of bacon fat from the pan, add the onion, and cook, stirring, until the onion is lightly browned, about 5 minutes.

3. Combine the flour, baking powder, salt, and paprika in a large bowl. Mix to blend, then make a well in the center of the flour mixture and add the buttermilk, melted butter, Cheddar, bacon, and onion. Mix gently with a wooden spoon. The dough will be slightly wet and sticky. Using a ½-cup dry measuring cup, portion the batter onto a baking sheet, leaving 1 inch or so between each biscuit. You will have about 6 biscuits.

4. Brush some of the reserved bacon fat on the top of each biscuit. Bake until the biscuits are golden brown and a toothpick inserted in the center of one comes out clean, 20 to 22 minutes.

SOUTHERN SIMPLE: This recipe doubles nicely. The biscuits can be baked ahead and frozen, then they can go from the freezer to the oven for a quick reheat.

SOUTHERN MOTHER: Place cards are a quick, fun craft for children to work on while the biscuits are baking.

BLUEBERRY CORNBREAD CUPCAKES

I could not ask for a better daughter than Daisy. She just oozes with fun and joy. She simply loves life. Sometimes, in the middle of the night, she'll run out of her room and ask, "Is it daylight yet?" She has no time for sleep! We love doing lots of things together, but one of our favorite things is to cook together. She would cook up a masterpiece of her own every day if I let her. The problem is that, so far at age seven, she hasn't mastered the cleanup like she has the creation. She's been making up her own recipes since she was three! At first, they weren't what you would call pleasingly edible. Now they're actually really tasty. Recently she came running into the kitchen saying, "Mommy, Mommy! I have this great recipe in my head, and I'm just going to have to bake it! I cannot handle it! I have to get it out of my head!" Now, how could I resist that?

So, these cornbread cupcakes got their name because of the word "cupcake." They're not all that sweet, but that name just sounds more enticing to a little girl who's actually quite picky about her food. These are a favorite at our house. Daisy loves to stir in the blueberries.

This recipe comes out making 14 muffins. If 13 makes a baker's dozen, then 14 surely make a "Simply Southern" dozen!"

Makes 14 cupcakes

1¾ CUPS YELLOW CORNMEAL

1½ CUPS SELF-RISING FLOUR

½ TEASPOON SALT

2 EGGS

1 CUP SUGAR

⅔ CUP COCONUT OIL

½ TEASPOON VANILLA EXTRACT

¾ CUP WHOLE MILK

¼ CUP BUTTERMILK

3 TABLESPOONS HONEY

2 CUPS BLUEBERRIES

MELTED BUTTER, FOR BRUSHING THE TOPS OF THE CUPCAKES

1. Preheat the oven to 400°F. Line 14 muffin cups with paper liners.

2. Stir together the cornmeal, flour, and salt in a large bowl. Using an electric mixer, cream together the eggs, sugar, coconut oil, and vanilla in a medium bowl.

3. Add the egg mixture to the cornmeal mixture and stir in the milk, buttermilk, and honey. Stir just until incorporated; do not overmix. Fold in the blueberries.

4. Fill each muffin cup with batter almost all the way to the rim. Bake until golden brown, 15 to 18 minutes. Brush the cupcake tops liberally with melted butter.

SOUTHERN MOTHER: Lots of stores these days have adorable cupcake paper liners. Let your little ones pick out their favorite style, and allow them to do the job of lining the muffin tins when it's time to put these yummy "cupcakes" in the oven.

SOUTHERN SIMPLE: For dessert or a late-night snack, crumble up one of these muffins into a glass of cold milk. Grab a long spoon and dig in. Heaven!

Citrus Cake with Lime Glaze

I baked this cake with my dear friend Craig Morgan, who's best known for his singing and songwriting. I just love his song "This Ole Boy." Craig is an all-around great guy. He served in the Army's 101st and 82nd Airborne Divisions, and even when he was well into his career in Nashville continued to serve in the Army Reserves for an additional nine years. He's worked for years with the USO, traveling the world to entertain the troops and bringing them a little piece of home to offer comfort. When we got together in the kitchen to make this cake, I could hardly get the batter in the pan—he spied those beaters, and there was no keeping him from licking them!

Makes 1 Bundt cake

CAKE

COOKING SPRAY

10 TABLESPOONS (1¼ STICKS) BUTTER, AT ROOM TEMPERATURE

1⅓ CUPS GRANULATED SUGAR

3 EGGS, AT ROOM TEMPERATURE

1 VANILLA BEAN, SPLIT OPEN

2 CUPS ALL-PURPOSE FLOUR

2 TEASPOONS BAKING POWDER

PINCH OF SALT

GRATED ZEST OF 2 ORANGES

⅔ CUP FRESH ORANGE JUICE

GLAZE

1¼ CUPS POWDERED SUGAR

ZEST AND JUICE OF 1 LIME

1. For the cake: Preheat the oven to 350°F. Coat a Bundt cake pan with cooking spray.

2. Using an electric mixer, cream the butter and granulated sugar. Beat in the eggs one at a time, making sure each is well incorporated before you add the next. Scrape the vanilla seeds out of the bean into the batter.

3. Sift the flour, baking powder, and salt into a medium bowl. Combine the orange zest and juice in a small bowl.

4. Add the flour mixture and orange juice to the creamed mixture in 5 alternating additions, beginning and ending with the flour, mixing just until incorporated after

each addition. Scrape any flour from the sides of the bowl. Do not overmix. Pour the batter into the Bundt pan.

5. Bake until a toothpick inserted in the center comes out clean, 45 to 55 minutes. Check with a toothpick every 10 minutes, starting at 35 minutes. Place on a cooling rack until the cake pulls away from the pan, about 20 minutes.

6. Meanwhile, make the glaze: Whisk the powdered sugar and lime juice in a small bowl until incorporated.

7. Flip the cake out of the pan onto a serving plate. Pour the glaze all over the top of the cake, letting it drip down the sides. Sprinkle with lime zest.

SOUTHERN SIMPLE: If Key limes are available, use those. If not, regular limes will do. However you get there, the combination of orange and lime in this cake has the bright flavor of a Florida vacation.

SOUTHERN MOTHER: I did it, you did it. We all did it: licked the beaters. People say you shouldn't eat cake batter because of the raw egg. If you're concerned about this, lick the whisk when you make the lime glaze instead!

Schlap Happy Bars

We're a couple of coffee drinkers, this here Mr. and Mrs. Schlapman. Sometimes an afternoon pick-me-up is in order. A tin of these butterscotch chocolate toffee bars stashed away in the kitchen is . . . well . . . nothing short of a home run with the Mister. With all the comings and goings around here, it's nice to sit down, take five, and be sweet.

Makes 12 bars

2 STICKS (½ POUND) BUTTER, AT ROOM TEMPERATURE

¾ CUP GRANULATED SUGAR

¾ CUP PACKED BROWN SUGAR

2 TEASPOONS VANILLA EXTRACT

2 LARGE EGGS

2¼ CUPS SELF-RISING FLOUR

1 CUP SEMISWEET CHOCOLATE CHUNKS

1 CUP BUTTERSCOTCH BAKING CHIPS

ONE 12-OUNCE BAG MINIATURE TOFFEE BARS, BROKEN INTO PIECES

1. Preheat the oven to 375°F. Grease a 9 x 13-inch baking pan.

2. Beat together the butter, granulated sugar, brown sugar, and vanilla in a large bowl until creamy. Add the eggs one at a time, stirring to combine after each one. Add the flour a little at a time and stir to combine after each addition. Stir in the chocolate chunks, butterscotch chips, and toffee chunks. Evenly spread the dough in the baking pan.

3. Bake until golden brown around the edges, 20 to 25 minutes. Let cool for 10 minutes. Cut into 12 bars and enjoy.

SOUTHERN SIMPLE: These chocolate toffee bars keep well for 3 days in an airtight container.

FRIENDLY COCONUT PIE

There comes a time when somebody you know needs a pie. You just know it when you see them—or when you've caught wind of something going on. This pie starts with a frozen pie-crust (whether your own or the grocer's), so it comes together quickly. I'm not saying pie can fix anything, but what I am saying is that taking a friend a pie—stopping in and showing up—well, that can only help.

Makes one 9-inch pie

2 EGGS

1 CUP SUGAR

4 TABLESPOONS (½ STICK) BUTTER, AT ROOM TEMPERATURE

1 HEAPING CUP SWEETENED FLAKED COCONUT

½ CUP MILK

PINCH OF SALT

1 TEASPOON VANILLA EXTRACT

ONE 9-INCH PIE SHELL

1. Preheat the oven to 325°F.

2. Using an electric mixer, beat together the eggs, sugar, and butter in a large bowl until well combined. Stir in the coconut, milk, salt, and vanilla.

3. Pour the batter into the pie shell and bake until the center is only the slightest bit jiggly and the crust is lightly browned, about 45 minutes. Let the pie cool for 10 minutes before serving.

SOUTHERN SIMPLE: If you know the intended recipient for this pie is a chocolate fan, sprinkle ½ cup semisweet chocolate chips into the mix before it goes in the oven.

Big-Batch Banana Pudding

Mealtime at my mama's and daddy's family homes were each different. My mama's family invited guests for dinner, while in my daddy's family whoever showed up was invited to eat. My mama tells the story of going to Sunday dinner at my daddy's house when they were dating. Amazed at the number around the table, she went back home and described the whole scene to her mother—including the gigantic bowl of banana pudding served at the end of dinner. Grams commented, "Why, that's not a bowl—that's a foot tub!"

Makes 10 to 12 servings

2 CUPS SUGAR

6 HEAPING TABLESPOONS SELF-RISING FLOUR

ONE 12-OUNCE CAN EVAPORATED MILK

4 EGG YOLKS PLUS 3 EGG WHITES

4 CUPS HOT WATER

2 PINCHES OF SALT

2 TEASPOONS VANILLA EXTRACT

ONE 11-OUNCE BOX VANILLA WAFERS

3 OR 4 BANANAS, CUT INTO ¼-INCH-THICK ROUNDS

ONE 7-OUNCE JAR MARSHMALLOW CRÈME

1. Preheat the oven to 350°F.

2. Combine the sugar, flour, and ½ can of evaporated milk in a large saucepan. Mix well. Add remaining evaporated milk and egg yolks. Slowly stir in the hot water. Heat the mixture over low heat, stirring constantly, until it thickens. Remove from the heat and add a pinch of salt and the vanilla.

3. Meanwhile, line the bottom of a 9 x 13-inch baking dish with the vanilla wafers. Then top with sliced bananas in an even layer.

4. Pour the pudding over the wafers and bananas.

5. Using an electric mixer, beat the egg whites and a pinch of salt to soft peaks. Add the marshmallow crème and beat to stiff peaks.

6. Evenly spread the meringue over the pudding and bake until the meringue is golden brown, 15 to 20 minutes. Let the pudding cool and set for 15 minutes before serving.

(continued)

SOUTHERN SIMPLE: Forget about scorching and get this pudding made quickly by mixing the sugar, flour, evaporated milk, hot water, and egg yolks in a large microwave-safe mixing bowl and cooking in the microwave. Cook the pudding on HIGH for 5 minutes. Stir and check for a thick consistency. Repeat, if necessary, cooking on HIGH in 3-minute increments until the desired thickness is reached. Remove from the microwave and stir in the vanilla and a pinch of salt.

DEBRA'S BANANA ICE CREAM

One of my mother's best friends, Debra Buchannan, is not only the definition of a true friend but a wonderful cook. We're always trading recipes with Debra! She and my mother walked in the three-day, sixty-mile Susan G. Komen Memorial breast cancer walk a few years ago in honor of my mother's mother, who died of breast cancer. They covered twenty miles a day for three days in a row. That's amazing! They have too many stories to count from those three very grueling days—some hilarious and some incredibly painful—but they ended with an even deeper friendship to show for it.

If you know you're going to make this ice cream—and truth be told, a day like that doesn't sneak up on you—put everything except the bananas in the refrigerator the night before. (The bananas can go into the fridge also, but don't be alarmed if this makes the skin go black!) When you're ready to churn the ice cream, just pour the milks and vanilla into freshly smashed bananas.

Makes 4 quarts

1 CUP SUGAR

1 QUART WHOLE MILK

TWO 14-OUNCE CANS SWEETENED CONDENSED MILK

ONE 12-OUNCE CAN EVAPORATED MILK

1 TABLESPOON VANILLA EXTRACT

5 RIPE BANANAS, MASHED

Mix all the ingredients together in a large bowl and pour the mixture into a 4-quart electric ice cream maker. Freeze according to the manufacturer's instructions.

SOUTHERN SIMPLE: Try 2 cups sweetened diced peaches or sweetened strawberries in place of the bananas in this recipe.

SOUTHERN MOTHER: Paper water cones usually available in the camping section make for good serving vessels for this easy ice cream.

GIRLFRIEND S'MORES

I feel blessed to count Natalie Hemby among my friends. She's the type of genuine gal who asks "How ya doing?" and truly wants to know how you are. Her thoughtful, creative nature inspires me. Natalie wrote both "Pontoon" and "Tornado," so that should give you an idea of what kind of bold, no-nonsense woman she is. We had so much fun cooking up these little jars of heaven on my cooking show, kitchen torches in hand!

These Mason jars filled with sautéed bananas, bittersweet chocolate, and graham crackers are topped with flambéed marshmallow crème and are such fun to serve when girlfriends come over for a big catch-up visit.

Makes 6 individual jars

2 TABLESPOONS BUTTER

3 BANANAS, SLICED

2 TABLESPOONS BROWN SUGAR

8 GRAHAM CRACKER SHEETS, CRUMBLED

8 OUNCES BITTERSWEET CHOCOLATE, MELTED

ONE 7-OUNCE JAR MARSHMALLOW CRÈME

1. Set an oven rack in the lowest position and preheat the broiler.

2. Heat the butter in a large skillet over medium heat. Add the bananas and brown sugar and cook, stirring occasionally, until the sugar dissolves and the bananas are well coated and tender, about 7 minutes.

3. Dividing evenly, layer the graham cracker crumbs, bananas, chocolate, and marshmallow crème in six 4-ounce glass Mason jars. Make sure the marshmallow is the top layer.

4. Place the jars on a rimmed baking sheet. Broil them until golden brown on top, about 5 minutes.

SOUTHERN SIMPLE: If you have one of those little torches used to make crème brûlée, use it to brown the marshmallow topping instead of broiling.

SOUTHERN MOTHER: Little girls and big girls alike love a chocolate treat. Make these ahead and top with a lid and with a gingham napkin displaying each guest's name. These little jars of yumminess are so super sticky that you'll need those napkins handy!

RUSSIAN TEA

I couldn't for the life of me figure out why this tea was called "Russian." And I'm a curious sort, so after a bit of research I found out that in Russia it was a tradition to serve tea sweetened with fruit jam or marmalade as opposed to serving it with cream as the British do. I always thought we called it "Russian" because it was so exotic, and Russia seemed so distant from our Appalachian hills.

Makes 1 gallon

4 FAMILY-SIZE TEA BAGS

2 CUPS SUGAR

2 CINNAMON STICKS

1 CUP ORANGE JUICE

2 CUPS PINEAPPLE JUICE

2 TEASPOONS LEMON JUICE

1. Bring 2 quarts water to a boil in a saucepan. Remove from the heat and add the tea bags. Steep for about 10 minutes.

2. Meanwhile, combine 1 quart water, the sugar, and cinnamon sticks in a medium saucepan to make a simple syrup. Cook over medium heat until the sugar is dissolved.

3. Discard the tea bags. In a large container, combine the tea, simple syrup, and fruit juices. Serve warm.

SOUTHERN SIMPLE: I also like this tea served chilled in the summer months. Place the tea in the freezer for 2 hours for a spiced fruit tea slushy.

CHAPTER 3

Music

For as long as I can remember, music has been part of my life. It has always been there, just like part of the family. Our home was always full of music. My mama has been the organist at church for more than forty years, and my daddy was the choir director for many years. My family was at church pretty much anytime the doors were open. I have the fondest memories of dinner on the grounds and Wednesday night fellowship suppers full of good food and song.

I loved playing the piano and began taking lessons (from somebody other than my mama) when I was eight years old. My teacher was a little old widowed lady named Mrs. Ogden. I loved learning to play, but I hated practicing my assigned lessons. I liked playing hymns and songs from my Olivia Newton John songbook instead. After a few years of lessons, I began to accompany my mother on the piano at church.

Like many girls, I would sway in front of my bedroom mirror and sing into my hairbrush. I knew all the songs from Alabama, Dolly Parton, Marie Osmond, Lionel Richie, and Andy Gibb. For a while, I might have even believed I was a member of the Bee Gees! I took every opportunity to sing for folks—whether in living room shows, at school, or in church plays. Anytime I could get an audience, I was singing. I am one of Barbara Mandrell's biggest fans, and when all the cousins would get together, we would put on variety shows with skits and songs just like hers. I would even belt out imaginary duets with Elvis. I knew in my heart that I just wanted to sing for people. I thought it was something I could do for them to make them laugh or just be happy. Still do.

In junior high I began to realize just how much singing meant to me. I started singing in talent contests all around the state of Georgia, and by high school I had started taking voice lessons from Mrs. Logan. She was tough on me, but I adored her. She made sure I practiced and didn't holler too much at football games. I also had two choral directors who gave me such encouragement to go for it. Ms. Rentz and Mr. Ivey will probably never know the confidence they instilled in me. I am so grateful for all they taught me and for the support and faith they offered me at such an impressionable age.

I don't know what I did to deserve such special parents! I won the lottery as far as that's concerned. They've always been my biggest fans. My sweet daddy would drive for hours and hours to take me to sing at civic functions, ball games, county fairs, even if it was to sing just one song—and never a complaint did he utter!

Both of my folks have always been incredibly encouraging to me about singing and performing. My mama would sneak little notes into my pockets or purse with the best advice: "You can do it!" "Don't be nervous!" "Believe in yourself!" I would find them when I was warming up, and suddenly I'd feel the butterflies settle down. If, heaven forbid, a day comes when I can no longer sing in tune, I know my parents will still be there to cheer me on.

Music has brought me so many amazing opportunities, from performing for presidents to my lifelong dream of winning a Grammy! I *believed* I would sing in RCA's famous Studio B—the same studio where Elvis recorded with the Jordanaires—and I *did*! Most of all, though, music has been my very close friend through heartbreak and grief—and through my greatest joys and celebrations.

OYSTERS WITH PEACH MIGNONETTE

In 1999 we signed our first record deal as Little Big Town. Phillip, Karen, Jimi, and I—along with the rest of the gang—went down to St. George Island, Florida. We celebrated for a whole week and devoured as many of the sweet, briny Apalachicola oysters as we could. My bandmates have always made fun of the way I pronounce the hometown of those tiny little morsels. Apparently I have an accent! This simple oyster preparation with champagne vinegar, shallots, and peaches has been a fine way to celebrate ever since.

Makes 24 oysters

1 CUP FINELY CHOPPED PEELED RIPE PEACHES

1 TABLESPOON MINCED SHALLOTS

¼ CUP CHAMPAGNE VINEGAR

1 TEASPOON MINCED FRESH CHIVES

¼ TEASPOON GROUND WHITE PEPPER

24 FRESH OYSTERS, SCRUBBED, SHUCKED, AND LOOSENED ON THE HALF SHELL

Combine the peaches, shallots, champagne vinegar, chives, and white pepper in a small bowl. Serve alongside the oysters.

SOUTHERN SIMPLE: When shucking an oyster, use a good-quality oyster knife. Use a hand towel or thick gardening gloves to protect your hands from cuts and abrasions. Keep oysters on ice. Never store them in a sealed bag; they will suffocate. You want them fresh and alive!

PECAN-STUFFED MUSHROOMS

These mushrooms are filled with buttery sautéed mushrooms and garlic combined with ground pecans and sharp pecorino cheese. These savory bites hold up well in a chafing dish and make a nice vegetarian addition to an hors d'oeuvres buffet at a cocktail party.

Makes 18 stuffed mushrooms

18 CREMINI (BABY BELLA) MUSHROOM CAPS PLUS 1 CUP QUARTERED CAPS

1 SMALL SHALLOT, PEELED

2 GARLIC CLOVES, PEELED

½ CUP PECAN PIECES OR ROUGHLY CHOPPED PECANS

3 TABLESPOONS BUTTER

1 TABLESPOON CHOPPED FRESH TARRAGON

SALT AND FRESHLY GROUND BLACK PEPPER

¼ CUP GRATED PECORINO CHEESE

1 TABLESPOON CHOPPED FRESH PARSLEY

OLIVE OIL, FOR DRIZZLING

1. Preheat the oven to 375°F.

2. Place the 18 mushroom caps on a baking sheet, top side down. Place the remaining 1 cup quartered mushrooms, the shallot, garlic, and pecans in a food processor and pulse until the mixture becomes a paste.

3. Melt the butter in a medium skillet over medium heat. Add the mushroom paste and cook for 2 to 3 minutes, stirring occasionally. Add the tarragon and season with salt and pepper.

4. Meanwhile, mix the pecorino and parsley in a small bowl. Season with salt and pepper.

5. Using a small spoon, fill each mushroom cap with the mushroom-pecan filling and top with the cheese mixture. Drizzle olive oil on top. Bake until golden brown, 12 to 15 minutes. Serve warm.

SOUTHERN SIMPLE: These mushroom hors d'oeuvres can be assembled a day in advance, refrigerated, and baked right before serving.

VIDALIA ONION DIP

Phillip Sweet was the voice that rounded out the LBT sound. Karen, Jimi, and I had begun singing together, but something was missing. We loved the sound we were making but felt like we needed a big low voice to round out what we had. As soon as Phillip joined, we knew our sound was complete. We all grew up singing harmony with our families, so the harmony came naturally and easily. Over the years we have sung harmony just about any which way you can sing it . . . and loved every bit of it!

I always like to have a snack ready when we get together for our brainstorming and songwriting sessions. When it comes to snacks, Phillip is a chip man, and his flavor of choice is sour cream and onion. Just the other night, he and I were sitting over some gloriously delicious onion dip the caterers had put in our dressing room. We desperately wanted to figure out what was in it so that we could make it. He loves food, and I love to make him happy by cooking for him, so this is my version. He is a fan of this baked-until-bubbling dip, and I am a fan of his!

Makes 3 cups

3 CUPS FINELY CHOPPED VIDALIA ONION

3 CUPS GRATED MEXICAN CHEESE BLEND

1 CUP MAYONNAISE

4 OUNCES CREAM CHEESE, AT ROOM TEMPERATURE

¼ TEASPOON RED PEPPER FLAKES

¼ TEASPOON SALT

1 TABLESPOON GRATED PARMESAN CHEESE

¼ TEASPOON PAPRIKA

TORTILLA CHIPS OR TOASTED BREAD SLICES, FOR SERVING

1. Preheat the oven to 350°F.

2. Combine the onion, cheese blend, mayonnaise, cream cheese, pepper flakes, and salt in a large bowl and mix well. Spread the mixture evenly in a small baking dish. Sprinkle the top with the Parmesan and paprika and bake for 25 minutes.

3. Serve warm with tortilla chips or toasted bread slices.

SOUTHERN SIMPLE: This also makes a doggone good filling for a grilled cheese sandwich!

SOUTHERN SIMPLE: Another favorite quick dip is Cheesy Peach Pepper Jelly Dip. Just combine 8 ounces room-temperature cream cheese and 6 ounces Texas peach habanero pepper jelly. Serve it on crackers and make some folks happy!

SOUTHERN MOTHER: This cheese dip is great with celery and carrot sticks. Dipping makes even vegetables fun.

SOUTHERN SKINNY: Use ⅓-less-fat cream cheese (Neufchâtel) and low-fat mayonnaise and serve with baked chips to cut a few calories.

CROSTINI AND BLACK-EYED PEA PUREE

I'm sure most folks know to eat black-eyed peas on New Year's Day for luck in the coming year. I'm not so much superstitious as I am a sucker for tradition. I also really love to sing the song of the New Year, "Auld Lang Syne."

Makes 6 servings

¼ CUP OLIVE OIL, PLUS MORE FOR DRIZZLING

3 THYME SPRIGS

½ TEASPOON RED PEPPER FLAKES

2 GARLIC CLOVES, SMASHED AND PEELED

1 BAY LEAF

ONE 15-OUNCE CAN BLACK-EYED PEAS, DRAINED AND RINSED

¼ CUP VEGETABLE BROTH

SALT AND FRESHLY GROUND BLACK PEPPER

1 BAGUETTE, THINLY SLICED ON THE DIAGONAL

1. Preheat the oven to 350°F.

2. Heat the ¼ cup olive oil in a medium saucepan over medium-high heat. Add the thyme, pepper flakes, garlic, and bay leaf. Cook, stirring occasionally, until the garlic is golden brown, about 2 minutes. Add the black-eyed peas and vegetable stock and bring to a boil. Reduce the heat to medium-low and simmer until the flavors have melded, about 10 minutes.

3. Discard the bay leaf and thyme stems and transfer the mixture to a blender. Puree until smooth, sprinkling in a little water if the mixture is too dry. Season with salt and black pepper to taste. Transfer to a bowl.

4. Arrange the bread on a baking sheet, drizzle the olive oil over the bread, and toast in the oven until golden brown, 7 to 8 minutes. Serve with the black-eyed pea puree.

SOUTHERN MOTHER: This thyme- and red-pepper-flecked black-eyed pea spread is a perfect match for Baked Oysters with Creamed Turnip Greens (page 204) for a New Year's party. The other part of the old New Year's dining lore says you should eat greens to ensure prosperity.

Slow-Cooker Chicken Quesadillas

This recipe for tender, stewed-down chicken quesadilla filling is one I come back to again and again. Sometimes work in the recording studio can run late, and this recipe is so forgiving that it's all the better even if dinner gets pushed back a couple of hours.

Makes 4 to 8 appetizer servings

2 TABLESPOONS OLIVE OIL, PLUS MORE FOR BRUSHING

4 BONELESS, SKINLESS CHICKEN BREASTS

1 CUP THINLY SLICED ONION

ONE 14-OUNCE CAN WHOLE PEELED TOMATOES, CRUSHED WITH YOUR HANDS

ONE 7-OUNCE CAN CORN KERNELS, DRAINED AND RINSED

2 JALAPEÑOS, SEEDED AND MINCED

1 AVOCADO, DICED SMALL

8 OUNCES CREAM CHEESE

2 TABLESPOONS CHOPPED FRESH CILANTRO

SALT AND FRESHLY GROUND BLACK PEPPER

FOUR 8-INCH TORTILLAS

2 CUPS SHREDDED MONTEREY JACK CHEESE

SALSA OR SOUR CREAM, FOR SERVING

1. Pour the olive oil into a slow cooker. Add the chicken, onion, tomatoes, corn, jalapeños, avocado, and cream cheese. Cover and cook on HIGH for 3 to 4 hours or on LOW for 6 to 8 hours, if desired.

2. Remove the chicken and shred it with two forks. Mash up the avocado pieces with a potato masher if they haven't cooked down. Stir the cilantro into the shredded chicken. Season with salt and pepper to taste. Mix well to coat the chicken with the sauce.

3. To make the quesadillas, heat a large skillet or griddle over medium-high heat. Sprinkle the Jack cheese on one half of a tortilla. Top with shredded chicken, then some more cheese. Fold the tortilla over the filling and brush olive oil on both sides. Place in the pan and cook for 3 to 4 minutes per side, until the quesadilla is a bit crispy and the cheese is melted. Repeat for all the tortillas and fillings.

4. Cut the quesadillas into wedges and serve with your favorite salsa or a dollop of sour cream.

SOUTHERN SIMPLE: Try these chicken quesadillas with Georgia Peach Salsa (page 65).

COOKIE PRESS CHEESE STRAWS

Cheese straws are perfect Southern tidbits to take to any gathering, whether it be a fancy shower, a church get-together, choir practice, or a musical jam session. Just think about how many you might need, then double that. These crisp, cayenne-tinged snack straws are simply addictive.

Makes about 12 dozen cheese straws

1 POUND SHARP CHEDDAR CHEESE, GRATED (ABOUT 4 CUPS)

2 STICKS PLUS 6 TABLESPOONS MARGARINE, AT ROOM TEMPERATURE

4 CUPS ALL-PURPOSE FLOUR

2 TEASPOONS SALT

1 TEASPOON PAPRIKA

¼ TEASPOON CAYENNE PEPPER, OR TO TASTE

1. Preheat the oven to 400°F. Line a rimmed baking sheet with parchment paper.

2. Blend the Cheddar and margarine in a large bowl. Sift the flour, salt, paprika, and cayenne into another large bowl. Gradually add the flour mixture to the cheese mixture and work it like a pastry dough, kneading until it's soft and well blended.

3. Using the "star" pattern of a cookie press, press out the dough into lengths down the baking sheet. Use a sharp knife to cut the lengths into pieces about 3 inches long.

4. Bake the cheese straws until golden brown, 9 to 10 minutes. Transfer them immediately to wax paper or a cooling rack. Cool completely, then store in an airtight container.

SOUTHERN SIMPLE: Try different shaped disks for different occasions: clovers for St. Patrick's Day, flowers for a spring fling, or little Christmas trees or stars for holiday play night. (I don't really know what bunco is, and I've never played bridge—but I hear these are good for those parties, too!)

The Cheese Straws are shown on the next page.

FRUIT AND CHEESE KEBABS

Before every show with Little Big Town, we gather together backstage in a little huddle for a quick prayer and some rowdy words of encouragement. Afterward, we pass around a honey bear, tilting back our heads, each taking a squeeze to soothe our throats before we go out and start singing. In that spirit, these bright fruit skewers drizzled with vanilla-infused honey have gotten to be a favorite snack that I bring to the studio when we're rehearsing or recording.

Makes 6 kebabs

You will need six 8-inch skewers.

3 NECTARINES, CUT INTO 6 WEDGES

18 MINT LEAVES

18 DRIED WHOLE APRICOTS

18 ONE-INCH CUBES GOUDA CHEESE

½ CUP HONEY

1 VANILLA BEAN, SPLIT LENGTHWISE

1. Place the ingredients on each of six 8-inch skewers in this order: nectarine section, mint leaf, dried apricot, cube of Gouda. Repeat twice on the same skewer.

2. Place the honey in a small bowl and scrape the vanilla seeds into the bowl. Stir to combine. Drizzle the skewers with vanilla honey and serve.

SOUTHERN MOTHER: These colorful kebabs are a mouthful of goodness, with protein, calcium, fiber, and vitamin C.

Opposite: Fruit and Cheese Kebabs with Cookie Press Cheese Straws, page 107.

Cucumber and Mint Soup

This chilled cream soup comes together in no time flat. My bandmates like this as an after-noon refresher. I'll whiz up a batch and have it ready in the fridge on the bus.

Makes 4 servings

One 10-ounce can condensed cream of celery soup

¾ cup milk

1 cup sour cream

2 English cucumbers, peeled and roughly chopped

1 avocado, roughly chopped

⅛ teaspoon freshly grated nutmeg

1 teaspoon celery salt

½ teaspoon salt

¼ teaspoon freshly ground black pepper

⅓ cup heavy (whipping) cream

¼ cup fresh mint leaves, plus sprigs for garnish

Place all the ingredients except the mint sprigs in a blender and blend until smooth. Chill for at least 2 hours. Serve cold, garnished with mint sprigs.

MUSHROOM BISQUE

I made this richly flavored, creamy soup with my dear friend Josh Turner on my cooking show. The whole show was about mushrooms: where they grow, how they grow, how to cook them. Josh has a deep, resonating voice. After we'd spent the entire day cooking and talking about mushrooms, he leaned in and said, "You know, I never really liked mushrooms, but that soup was good!" What a sweet guy! He didn't want to hurt my feelings. A true Southern gentleman. It does go to show, though—this bisque is quite good!

Makes 4 servings

2 TABLESPOONS BUTTER

2 TABLESPOONS OLIVE OIL

½ CUP FINELY CHOPPED ONION

2 TABLESPOONS MINCED GARLIC

1½ POUNDS SHIITAKE AND CREMINI (BABY BELLA) MUSHROOMS, STEMMED AND THINLY SLICED

SALT AND FRESHLY GROUND BLACK PEPPER

4 CUPS CHICKEN BROTH

½ CUP HEAVY (WHIPPING) CREAM

3 TABLESPOONS SHERRY OR APPLE CIDER

1. Heat the butter and olive oil in a large pot over medium heat until the butter is melted. Add the onion and cook until translucent, about 2 minutes. Add the garlic and cook for 1 minute.

2. Add all the mushrooms and cook until soft, 10 to 12 minutes. Season with salt and pepper to taste. Set aside some of the sautéed mushrooms to use as a garnish.

3. Add the stock, cream, and sherry, bring to a simmer, and cook for 5 minutes. Puree the soup in a blender until smooth.

4. Pour the soup into bowls and top each with a garnish of sautéed mushrooms.

> SOUTHERN SIMPLE: Use whatever combination of mushrooms you like or that look particularly nice at the market.
>
> Portobello mushrooms are simply mature cremini mushrooms. When a mushroom has exposed gills beneath the cap, it will have a deeper, more earthy flavor. Shiitakes have very woody stems and parasol-shaped caps that range from khaki to dark brown. They're the mushrooms that look like the dancing mushrooms in the musical animated classic *Fantasia*.

BAKED ONION RINGS WITH HOT RANCH DIP

I have sung at every kind of fair or festival imaginable. Over the years I developed a weakness for fried festival food from local vendors. These crunchy onion rings are baked with a crumb coating and fulfill my craving for festival food without the greasy guilt. Speaking of guilt, this crazy dip is a guilty pleasure.

Makes 4 servings

ONION RINGS

4 VIDALIA ONIONS, SLICED INTO ¼-INCH-THICK RINGS

5 CUPS BUTTERMILK

1 CUP ITALIAN-STYLE BREADCRUMBS

1 CUP RITZ CRACKER CRUMBS (FROM 1 SLEEVE, ABOUT 31 CRACKERS)

1½ TEASPOONS SEASONED SALT

½ TEASPOON FRESHLY GROUND BLACK PEPPER

¼ TEASPOON CAYENNE PEPPER

½ TEASPOON PAPRIKA

HOT RANCH DIP

½ CUP PACKED BROWN SUGAR

⅛ TEASPOON FRESHLY GRATED NUTMEG

6 TABLESPOONS HOT SAUCE

½ CUP STORE-BOUGHT BUTTERMILK RANCH SALAD DRESSING

1. Make the onions: Place the onions and buttermilk in a large bowl and refrigerate for 1 to 2 hours.

2. Preheat the oven to 450°F. Spray a baking sheet with nonstick spray.

3. Combine the breadcrumbs, Ritz cracker crumbs, seasoned salt, black pepper, cayenne, and paprika in a medium bowl. Pour half the breadcrumb mixture into a shallow bowl, reserving the rest to add when the breadcrumbs in the bowl get wet and clumpy.

4. Working in batches, dredge the soaked onions in the breadcrumbs, coating both sides. Place as many onion rings as will fit in a single layer on the baking sheet and bake until golden brown, 12 to 15 minutes. Repeat to make the rest of the onion rings.

5. Make the hot ranch dip: Combine the brown sugar, nutmeg, hot sauce, and ¼ cup water in a small saucepan. Cook over medium heat until the sugar is dissolved. Remove from the heat and stir in the buttermilk ranch dressing.

6. Serve the hot ranch dip with the baked onion rings.

SOUTHERN SIMPLE: Use some of the buttermilk left over from soaking the onion rings to make Buttermilk Mashed Potatoes (page 158) or to soak the breadcrumbs in Turkey Meatballs (page 128). The flavored buttermilk will add a bump of onion flavor.

ROASTED TOMATOES WITH ROSEMARY AND GARLIC

We were singing in a recording studio once, and there were some peak-of-the-season ripe tomatoes set out for lunch in the break room kitchen. Both Karen and I are crazy for tomatoes in the summer. We started eating them with just a sprinkle from a shaker set on the table. We just couldn't stop eating them. We went on and on about how sweet these tomatoes were and how they must be a special variety grown in the region. After several tomatoes, we realized somebody had put sugar in the saltshaker! Joke's on us!

When tomato season is at its peak, these long-roasted tomatoes are no joke. They're perfect slipped inside a sandwich or tossed in with pasta or salad.

Makes 4 servings

1 POUND TOMATOES, CORED AND CUT CROSSWISE INTO ½-INCH SLICES

BASIL OLIVE OIL, FOR DRIZZLING (SEE SOUTHERN SIMPLE)

3 TABLESPOONS CHOPPED FRESH ROSEMARY

SALT AND FRESHLY GROUND BLACK PEPPER

4 GARLIC CLOVES, SMASHED

1. Preheat the oven to 325°F. Line a rimmed baking sheet with parchment paper.

2. Place the tomato slices on the baking sheet and generously drizzle with basil olive oil. Sprinkle the rosemary on top and season with salt and pepper to taste. Place the garlic around the tomatoes. Bake until the garlic is deep golden and the tomatoes have cooked way down and begun to brown, about 2 hours.

SOUTHERN SIMPLE: To make your own basil oil, gently warm extra-virgin olive oil over low heat with ¼ cup chopped fresh basil leaves. Heat for 5 minutes, then let sit for 1 hour. Strain the oil and store in a bottle with a tight-fitting cap for up to 1 week in the refrigerator.

MOTHER'S DAY ASPARAGUS CASSEROLE

Now, all the members of the Little Big Town are mamas and papas. Karen and Jimi have an adorable little boy, Elijah; Phillip and his wife, Rebecca, have a beautiful little girl, Penelopi; and Steve and I have our darling Daisy.

We all say that if it weren't for Karen's tenacity and care of our business, we wouldn't be a band. She really enjoys the business side of things, and she is great at being the band's liaison. She and I have walked hand in hand through a lot, sometimes scared and not knowing what the outcome would be. Thankfully, though, we've always made it through together. Besides being a great friend and businesswoman, she's a wonderful mom. She loves and adores her little man to pieces. I'm so happy she's able to live out her dream of being a mommy.

A spring Mother's Day brunch, when asparagus is in season, is just the right occasion to make this dish.

Makes 4 servings

1 STICK PLUS 2 TABLESPOONS UNSALTED BUTTER

1 CUP RITZ CRACKER CRUMBS (FROM 1 SLEEVE, ABOUT 31 CRACKERS)

2 HEAPING TABLESPOONS ALL-PURPOSE FLOUR

2 CUPS MILK

8 OUNCES VELVEETA CHEESE, CUBED OR SHREDDED

3 CUPS (1-INCH) SLICES ASPARAGUS

1 CUP THINLY SLICED MUSHROOM CAPS OF YOUR CHOICE

1 CUP FROZEN PEAS

4 OUNCES PIMENTO, DRAINED AND CHOPPED

1 CUP MINCED ONION

½ TEASPOON SALT

¼ TEASPOON FRESHLY GROUND BLACK PEPPER

1. Preheat the oven to 350°F.

2. Melt 1 stick of the butter in a small saucepan over low heat. Mix in the crushed crackers and set aside.

3. Melt the remaining 2 tablespoons butter in a large saucepan over medium heat. Add the flour and whisk until smooth. Slowly whisk in the milk and keep whisking until thickened. Whisk in the Velveeta. When the mixture is smooth and melted, add the asparagus, mushrooms, peas, pimento, and onion and season with the

salt and pepper. Stir and pour into a 2-quart baking dish. Top with the onion and crushed cracker mixture.

4. Bake until bubbling and golden brown on top, about 30 minutes.

SOUTHERN SIMPLE: This casserole can be assembled a day ahead. Cover and refrigerate the casserole until ready to bake, then allow to come to room temperature for 30 minutes before baking.

To store asparagus spears in the refrigerator, trim 1 inch from the bottom and stand them up in 1 inch of water.

Speaking of Mother's Day, mothers always have their babies' best interests at heart. When I was fifteen, I was invited to be the entertainment for the high school beauty pageant intermission. It was quite an honor, and Mama took me shopping to get a new outfit for it, which was a big treat. I wore a beautiful silver metallic blouse with a black tank top underneath and silky black pants. It came time for intermission. My time to shine! I proudly walked out onstage, a little bit nervous. I was always a little bit nervous when I walked onstage—and I *still* am today. I began singing "Nobody Loves Me Like You Do" to my cassette musical track accompaniment. It was going very well until I noticed Mama in the fourth row doing contortions with her body, crossing her arms across her chest, and looking completely distraught. What in the world was she trying to tell me? Well, the show must go on, so I continued and figured I would talk to Mama about whatever craziness was happening to her when I was done entertaining the big crowd. I had work to do!

I finished to roaring applause from the audience. I bowed and walked offstage. Mama met me just as I walked out from behind the curtain. She still had that awful look on her face. She said, "Oh baby! You forgot your shirt!" I looked down in great fear that I had walked out there naked and looked back up at Mama totally confused. She said, "Your undershirt!!!" *Oh Gussie!* I had forgotten to put that very crucial black tank top on under the transparent metallic shirt. Yep, I said *transparent*. Without the black tank, all that was visible in the bright stage lights was my very white strapless bra!!! I pulled a Madonna even before there was such thing! Still a Most Embarrassing Moment!

Bacon, Lettuce, and Fried Green Tomato Sandwich with Garlic Mayo

LBT is the shorthand version of our band's name. I think this stack of down-home flavors could be our official band sandwich. A bandwich, even! An LBT BLT!

Makes 4 sandwiches

FRIED TOMATOES

COCONUT OIL, FOR FRYING

1½ CUPS CORNMEAL

1 TEASPOON PAPRIKA

½ TEASPOON CAYENNE PEPPER

1 TEASPOON SALT, PLUS MORE FOR SPRINKLING

½ TEASPOON FRESHLY GROUND BLACK PEPPER

1 CUP ALL-PURPOSE FLOUR

3 EGGS

2 GREEN TOMATOES, CUT INTO ¼-INCH-THICK SLICES

GARLIC MAYO

2 TABLESPOONS MINCED GARLIC

½ CUP MAYONNAISE

1 TABLESPOON LEMON JUICE

SALT AND FRESHLY GROUND BLACK PEPPER

SANDWICHES

8 SLICES MULTIGRAIN BREAD, TOASTED

12 SLICES BACON, COOKED

ICEBERG LETTUCE

1. Make the fried tomatoes: Heat coconut oil in a large cast-iron skillet over medium heat to 350°F. When melted, the oil should reach halfway up the pan.

2. Combine the cornmeal, paprika, cayenne, salt, and pepper in a shallow dish. Place the flour in a second shallow dish. Lightly beat the eggs in a third shallow dish. Dredge the tomato slices first in the flour, then the eggs, then the seasoned cornmeal. Add the breaded tomatoes to the oil and fry for about 3 minutes on each side, until golden brown. Remove and drain on paper towels. Sprinkle with salt.

3. Make the garlic mayo: Mix the garlic, mayonnaise, and lemon juice in a small bowl. Season with salt and pepper to taste.

4. Assemble the sandwiches: Spread the garlic mayonnaise on 4 of the toast slices and make sandwiches using the bacon, lettuce, and fried green tomatoes.

SOUTHERN SKINNY: If you want to cut down on the fat in this sandwich, use turkey bacon and reduced-fat mayonnaise. The green tomatoes can also be "oven-fried" using the method in Baked Onion Rings (page 114).

HAM HASH BROWNS AND BAKED EGGS

Jimi Westbrook is the playful spirit of Little Big Town. He's a sweet ole country boy from Sumiton, Alabama, a little town where the biggest event is the annual Frog Festival held each October. Jimi and I have a long-standing but loving sense of competition between the two of us. You know the old saying "Anything boys can do, girls can do better"? Well, that's me and Jimi. I love him dearly. We once had the treat and pleasure of flying with the famous Blue Angels. Jimi went first, then Phillip, then me. Karen stayed on the ground because she happens to be the logical one in the band. When it was time for me to take off, the pilot asked me how many G's I wanted to pull. I promptly asked him, "How many did Jimi pull?" He said, "7.3." So I said, "Okay, then, 7.3!" I have so much fun with Jimi; he's like my brother. He's also a breakfast fan, so I make this dish for him. He loves salty country ham with onion and pepper hash browns, topped with a sunny-side-up baked egg. Plus, he knows the difference between city ham and country ham!

Makes 4 servings

1 POUND RUSSET (BAKING) POTATOES

2 TABLESPOONS BUTTER

1 TABLESPOON OLIVE OIL

½ CUP FINELY CHOPPED ONION

½ CUP FINELY DICED RED BELL PEPPER

1 POUND COOKED COUNTRY HAM, DICED

4 LARGE EGGS

SALT AND FRESHLY GROUND BLACK PEPPER

1. Preheat the oven to 375°F.

2. Peel the potatoes and grate them on the large holes of a box grater or shredding disk of a food processor. Place the potatoes in a large bowl of cold water to prevent browning.

3. Heat the butter in a large skillet and add the olive oil. Add the onion and cook, stirring occasionally, until translucent, 3 to 4 minutes.

4. Remove the potatoes from the water and squeeze out any excess liquid. Drain the potatoes on paper towels.

5. Add the potato to the skillet and cook for 3 minutes. Add the bell pepper and ham and cook for 2 minutes.

6. Divide the mixture among four 7-ounce ramekins and set the ramekins on a rimmed baking sheet. Crack an egg into each ramekin on top of the hash mixture and bake until the eggs are cooked through but still runny, about 20 minutes. Season with salt and black pepper.

SOUTHERN SIMPLE: "City" ham is smoked and wet cured. "Country" ham is dry-cured and smoked.

SOUTHERN SIMPLE: If you need a time-saver for this recipe, use a 1-pound package of refrigerated shredded potatoes from the grocer.

SOUTHWEST TORTILLA ROLL-UPS

I was born in the Southeast, but I think my taste buds came from the Southwest!

Makes 10 servings

16 OUNCES CREAM CHEESE, AT ROOM TEMPERATURE

2 TABLESPOONS DRY HIDDEN VALLEY RANCH DRESSING MIX

1 TABLESPOON SOUTHWEST-STYLE SEASONING

ONE 15-OUNCE CAN BLACK BEANS, DRAINED AND RINSED

ONE 15-OUNCE CAN WHOLE KERNEL CORN, DRAINED

ONE 4.5-OUNCE CAN DICED GREEN CHILES, DRAINED

2 CUPS SHREDDED MOZZARELLA CHEESE

TEN 8-INCH FLOUR TORTILLAS

SALSA, FOR SERVING

1. Stir the cream cheese, ranch dressing mix, and Southwest seasoning in a large bowl until combined. Stir in the beans, corn, chiles and mozzarella.

2. Spread ½ cup of the mixture all over one side of each tortilla. Roll up the tortillas and chill for at least 30 minutes. Slice on the diagonal and serve with your favorite salsa.

> SOUTHERN SIMPLE: Cut these Southwestern-spiced wraps crosswise into 1-inch-wide pinwheels for a make-ahead party snack.
>
> SOUTHERN MOTHER: These roll-ups make fun finger food for kids and grown-ups.

SUNDAY POT ROAST

It can make your head spin, seeing how fast my little family can change out of "church clothes" and into "lounging clothes" when we get home on Sunday mornings. When we get home and open the door, the smell of this pot roast is a big "welcome home!" I like to put this roast on to cook around midnight on Saturday. By lunchtime on Sunday it is perfectly done.

Makes 4 to 6 servings

ONE 3- TO 4-POUND CHUCK ROAST

1 PACKET LIPTON FRENCH ONION SOUP MIX

1 LARGE ONION, QUARTERED

6 CARROTS, ROUGHLY CHOPPED

TWO 10.75-OUNCE CANS CONDENSED CREAM OF MUSHROOM SOUP

½ CUP MILK

Coat the roast with the onion soup mix and place it in a slow cooker. Add the onion and carrots. Spread the canned soup over and around the roast. Pour the milk on top and cook it on LOW for 12 hours. The meat will be falling apart.

SOUTHERN SIMPLE: I serve this tender chuck roast with Buttermilk Mashed Potatoes (page 158) or over rice.

SOUTHERN SIMPLE: It may be tempting to crank the heat up to high. Don't do it— the meat needs the time to cook slow and low, and too much heat will cause the mushroom gravy to scorch.

TURKEY MEATBALLS

Martina McBride and I made these on my cooking show, Kimberly's Simply Southern. *Martina is a wonderful cook, and we had such fun in the kitchen together. Pecans give these meatballs a deep, rich flavor. Sometimes ground turkey can be a little dry, but sourdough bread soaked in buttermilk keeps these meatballs moist.*

Makes 12 meatballs

1 CUP TORN SOURDOUGH BREAD, FROM ABOUT 6 SLICES, CRUSTS REMOVED

½ CUP BUTTERMILK

1 POUND GROUND TURKEY

⅓ CUP PECAN PIECES, FINELY CHOPPED

1 EGG

1 TEASPOON ONION POWDER

2 GARLIC CLOVES, MINCED

1 TABLESPOON FINELY CHOPPED FRESH PARSLEY

1 TABLESPOON FINELY CHOPPED FRESH BASIL

½ TEASPOON SALT

¼ TEASPOON FRESHLY GROUND BLACK PEPPER

¼ CUP VEGETABLE OIL

HOMEMADE TOMATO SAUCE (PAGE 159) OR YOUR FAVORITE TOMATO SAUCE

1. Preheat the oven to 350°F. Line a rimmed baking sheet with foil.

2. Place the bread in a small bowl and add the buttermilk to soak.

3. Combine the turkey, pecans, egg, onion powder, garlic, parsley, basil, salt, and pepper in a large bowl. Remove the bread from the buttermilk and gently squeeze out the excess liquid. Add the soaked bread to the turkey mixture and discard the buttermilk. Using your hands, mix all the ingredients well. Divide the mixture into 12 portions and roll each one into a meatball.

4. Heat the oil in large heavy-bottomed skillet over medium-high heat. Working in batches, fry the meatballs until golden brown on all sides, 2 to 3 minutes. Drain the meatballs on paper towels.

5. Place the meatballs on the prepared baking sheet and bake until thoroughly browned and cooked through, 10 to 12 minutes. Serve with warm tomato sauce on top or on the side for dipping.

SOUTHERN SIMPLE: Use these meatballs in a big sub sandwich with tomato sauce and provolone cheese. Pack 'em up for a picnic. My Schlappy loves meatball subs!

Grilled Brioche with Warm Honey Strawberries

Sugarland's Kristian Bush is a big pal of mine. I made Kristian this toast topped with fresh thyme-infused strawberries and honey. He loved it so much he joked he was going to change his name to Warm Honey Strawberry Bush! He could get away with it, too, because he's so sweet.

Makes 4 servings

2 TABLESPOONS HONEY

1 VANILLA BEAN, SPLIT LENGTHWISE

1 QUART STRAWBERRIES, GREEN CAPS REMOVED

2 THYME SPRIGS

4 THICK SLICES BRIOCHE BREAD

MELTED BUTTER, FOR BRUSHING

WHIPPED CREAM (OPTIONAL)

1. Preheat the grill to medium-low.

2. Place the honey in a small bowl, scrape in the vanilla seeds, and mix well.

3. Make a foil packet to hold the strawberries and top them with the honey-vanilla mixture and the thyme. Seal the packet and grill it for 10 to 12 minutes, until the strawberries are soft.

4. Brush the brioche slices with melted butter and grill until golden brown on both sides, about 1 minute 30 seconds per side.

5. Serve the brioche topped with warm strawberries. If desired, dollop with whipped cream.

SOUTHERN SIMPLE: Do not wash strawberries before you store them; wash them just before you plan to use them.

SOUTHERN SIMPLE: Brioche is a rich, slightly sweet bread made with butter and eggs in the dough.

SOUTHERN MOTHER: Strawberries are an excellent source of vitamin C and also contain iron and potassium. My little Daisy is crazy about them.

MAMA'S TEA CAKES

My mama likes to mother the whole band. If we're playing within a three-hour radius of my hometown, she and Daddy will come for the show. One of the things all the bandmates and crew look forward to are Mama's Tea Cakes. Whether the tea cakes should be iced or not is a big debate not only in our family but also among the band members and their children. Daisy, her cousins, and her playmates always vote for icing, while the grown folks opt for plain. But there's no debate about whether the kids love to help frost these sugar cookie–like tea cakes. They do!

Makes 3 dozen cookies

TEA CAKES

1¼ CUPS GRANULATED SUGAR

⅔ CUP VEGETABLE SHORTENING

2 EGGS

1 TABLESPOON MILK

1 TEASPOON VANILLA EXTRACT

3 CUPS SELF-RISING FLOUR, SIFTED

PINCH OF SALT

ICING

6 TABLESPOONS BUTTER, MELTED

3½ CUPS POWDERED SUGAR, SIFTED

¼ TEASPOON SALT

1 TEASPOON VANILLA EXTRACT

3 TO 4 TABLESPOONS HALF-AND-HALF

1. Make the tea cakes: Preheat the oven to 375°F. Line a baking sheet with parchment paper.

2. Cream the granulated sugar, shortening, eggs, milk, and vanilla in a large bowl. Combine the flour and salt in a medium bowl. Add the flour mixture to the wet mixture, mixing until a dough forms. Knead the dough a few times to make it come together.

3. Roll the dough out on a floured surface to a ⅛-inch thickness. Use a 2-inch round cutter to cut out cookies, then place them on the baking sheet, leaving space between each cookie. Bake until golden brown, 8 to 10 minutes. Transfer to cooling racks. Roll out any dough scraps to cut out and bake more cookies.

4. Make the icing: Stir together the melted butter, powdered sugar, and salt. Mix in the vanilla, then slowly stir in 3 tablespoons half-and-half. Add more if needed to reach a proper frosting consistency.

5. Frost the tea cakes while they're still slightly warm, which will help the icing spread and glaze the tea cake. Set to dry on the cooling rack for 30 minutes. (Or if you can't stand it, eat one right away!)

6. Store in an airtight container for up to 1 week. Use wax paper between layers, if needed.

CHOCOLATE CHERRY COLA CAKE

I love to celebrate birthdays with the crew and my bandmates. When we're on the road, it's nice to have the band family celebrate. Jimi's birthday falls at the end of October, and I sometimes make this silly chocolate cherry cola cake for him, decorating the top with chocolate cherry cordials or gummy candies. I always let him choose what he's got a hankering for, and it's often this.

Make one 9 x 13-inch cake

CAKE

1 BOX DEVIL'S FOOD CAKE MIX

1 CUP (8 OUNCES) CHERRY COLA

½ CUP VEGETABLE OIL

3 EGGS

1 TEASPOON VANILLA EXTRACT

ONE 10-OUNCE JAR MARASCHINO CHERRIES, DRAINED (RESERVE ¼ CUP OF THE LIQUID) AND CHOPPED

FROSTING

⅓ CUP BUTTER, AT ROOM TEMPERATURE

4½ CUPS POWDERED SUGAR, SIFTED

¼ CUP MILK

1½ TEASPOONS VANILLA EXTRACT

ONE 7-OUNCE JAR MARSHMALLOW CRÈME

18 FRESH CHERRIES, CHOPPED

1. Make the cake: Preheat the oven to 350°F. Grease a 9 x 13-inch cake pan.

2. Whisk together the cake mix, cherry cola, oil, eggs, vanilla, and the reserved cherry juice in a large bowl until well combined. Stir in the maraschino cherries. Pour the batter into the cake pan and bake until a toothpick inserted in the center comes out clean, 30 to 35 minutes. Cool in the pan for at least 1 hour.

3. Make the frosting: Using an electric mixer, beat the butter in a large bowl until fluffy. Gradually add 2 cups of the powdered sugar. Slowly beat in the milk and vanilla, then beat in the remaining powdered sugar. Add the marshmallow crème and mix well, then fold in the cherries. Frost the cooled cake in the pan.

(continued)

SOUTHERN SIMPLE: If I make this in July I'll use fresh pitted cherries in the frosting for a bit of tang and garnish the top with fresh cherries as well. Jimi and I can eat our weight in fresh cherries during the summer. We're always bringing them on the bus to share. If it isn't cherry season, I use bright red maraschino cherries in the frosting.

SOUTHERN MOTHER: For a really silly decoration for a kid's party, top the cake with some cherry- and cola bottle–shaped gummy candies.

Hummingbird Cake

I love writing songs with my dear friend Natalie Hemby and all of our bandmates. Over the course of a long day we wrote the song "Night Owl" while polishing off just about a whole one of these banana, pineapple, and ginger pecan cakes. The song is a romantic lullaby about two lovebirds finding their way back to each other.

Makes one 9-inch triple-layer cake

CAKE

COOKING SPRAY

3 MEDIUM-RIPE BANANAS, FINELY CHOPPED

1½ CUPS FINELY CHOPPED FRESH PINEAPPLE

1 CUP PECANS, FINELY CHOPPED

2 CUPS PACKED LIGHT BROWN SUGAR

1 CUP VEGETABLE OIL

3 EGGS

1 TEASPOON VANILLA EXTRACT

3½ CUPS ALL-PURPOSE FLOUR, SIFTED

1¼ TEASPOONS BAKING SODA

1 TEASPOON GROUND CINNAMON

½ TEASPOON GROUND GINGER

1 TEASPOON SALT

FROSTING

16 OUNCES CREAM CHEESE, AT ROOM TEMPERATURE

2 STICKS (½ POUND) UNSALTED BUTTER, AT ROOM TEMPERATURE

2 TEASPOONS VANILLA EXTRACT

8 CUPS POWDERED SUGAR, SIFTED

GRATED ZEST OF 1 LEMON

DRIED BANANA CHIPS AND DRIED PINEAPPLE, FOR GARNISH (OPTIONAL)

1. Make the cake: Preheat the oven to 350°F. Coat three 9-inch cake pans with cooking spray.

2. Using a whisk, combine the bananas, pineapple, pecans, sugar, oil, eggs, and vanilla in a large bowl and mix until blended well. Sift the flour, baking soda, cinnamon, ginger, and salt into the bowl. Fold in with a rubber spatula until evenly blended. Divide the batter evenly among the 3 pans.

(continued)

3. Bake until a toothpick inserted in the center of each cake comes out clean, 25 to 30 minutes. Let the cakes cool in the pans for 10 minutes. Then invert the cakes onto cooling racks and let cool completely.

4. Make the frosting: Using an electric mixer, beat the cream cheese, butter, and vanilla in a large bowl until fluffy. Add the powdered sugar, 1 cup at a time, and blend well. Beat in the lemon zest. The frosting should be creamy and fluffy.

5. To ice the cake, place one layer bottom side up on a dessert plate or cake stand. Top with ¾ cup frosting, spreading it evenly to the edges of the cake. Repeat with a second cake layer and another ¾ cup frosting. Add the top layer and spread the remaining frosting on the top and sides of the cake. Arrange banana chips and dried pineapple on top of the cake for a garnish, if desired.

SOUTHERN SIMPLE: Tuck little strips of wax paper under the bottom edges of the cake to keep the plate clean while you spread the frosting.

CHAPTER 4

Home

When my husband, Steve, and I were house shopping several years ago, as soon as we drove up the driveway and walked into what is now our house, we knew this would be home. Everything about it was perfect—except the tiny little kitchen. For someone who loves to cook, it was quite the cramped space. We put that tiny little kitchen to big use for a long time but always dreamed of expanding it someday. Steve, who is a gifted carpenter, even drew up specific plans early on for how our dream kitchen would be laid out.

Well, a little song about a boat brought life to that dream: after "Pontoon" hit, we embarked on a big remodel. Our dream kitchen became a reality, and it is just that—the kitchen I'd dreamed of since I was a teenager. Steve's floor plan was brilliant, and it looks like it was always there as it is now. As most remodels go, ours took longer than we had anticipated. When the day finally came to move in, I happened to be home alone. Daisy and Steve had gone to visit family. I spent nine hours all by myself that day unpacking with happy tears just a flowin'. I pretty much had church up in there! I was praising the Lord for my new little piece of heaven. I still do that—and often. It really means so much to me.

Our kitchen is the heart and soul of our home. It's where we gather. It's cozy and warm . . . and it usually smells yummy. Sometimes it's perfectly neat (I can be a neat freak), and sometimes—especially when Daisy and I cut loose—it's a beautiful disaster. It's not my natural tendency to just let the sugar and flour fly, but I've learned to let go of some of my quirkiness about being neat, because the memories are always worth the extra cleanup. I wouldn't trade one single flour-y nose for a spotless kitchen.

CAESAR'S COUSIN'S SALAD BITES

I add a touch of molasses to the Caesar salad–like dressing to add some earthy sweetness. Once the dressing is tossed with crunchy croutons, tomato, and cucumber, I parcel out the salad into romaine lettuce leaves. I like to eat these right out of hand while cooking outside on the grill.

Makes 6 servings

CROUTONS

2 CUPS DICED DAY-OLD BREAD

2 TABLESPOONS OLIVE OIL

1 TEASPOON KOSHER SALT

CAESAR DRESSING

¼ CUP OLIVE OIL

¼ CUP VEGETABLE OIL

2 TABLESPOONS RICE VINEGAR

2 TEASPOONS MOLASSES

1 TEASPOON DIJON MUSTARD

1 TEASPOON FRESH LEMON JUICE

½ TEASPOON MINCED GARLIC

1 TEASPOON KOSHER SALT

¾ TEASPOON GROUND WHITE PEPPER

¼ TEASPOON MUSTARD POWDER

¼ TEASPOON SUGAR

1 EGG

SALAD BITES

12 LARGE ROMAINE LETTUCE LEAVES (FROM ABOUT 2 HEADS), WASHED

2 CUPS CHERRY TOMATOES, QUARTERED

½ ENGLISH CUCUMBER, CHOPPED

¼ CUP CHOPPED FRESH PARSLEY

¼ TEASPOON FRESHLY GROUND BLACK PEPPER

1. Make the croutons: Preheat the oven to 375°F.

2. Toss the bread cubes with the olive oil and salt in a bowl. Spread the bread evenly on a rimmed baking sheet and bake until golden brown, 5 to 8 minutes.

(continued)

3. Make the Caesar dressing: Whisk together all the ingredients until emulsified, or use a blender to make it easier. Refrigerate for at least 30 minutes before using.

4. Assemble the salad bites: Place the lettuce leaves on a platter. Toss the tomatoes, cucumbers, parsley, pepper, croutons, and dressing in a salad bowl. Fill the lettuce leaves with the salad mixture.

SOUTHERN SIMPLE: This is a nice choice for backyard entertaining. A platter of these colorful individual salads looks very inviting.

Citrus Salad with Poppy Seed Dressing

I was down in Florida when the citrus groves were in bloom and if I closed my eyes I would have sworn I was in a perfume bottle. This salad is a tangle of citrus flavors and smooth, buttery avocado over lettuce—topped with a honey dressing and toasted almonds.

Makes 4 servings

2 BLOOD ORANGES, SEGMENTED

2 NAVEL ORANGES, SEGMENTED

1 POMELO OR RUBY RED GRAPEFRUIT, SEGMENTED

1 AVOCADO, DICED

⅓ CUP SLICED ALMONDS, TOASTED

1½ TEASPOONS POPPY SEEDS

JUICE OF 1 LEMON

¼ CUP OLIVE OIL

1 TABLESPOON HONEY

SALT AND FRESHLY GROUND BLACK PEPPER

1 HEAD BIBB OR BUTTER LETTUCE, TORN INTO BITE-SIZE PIECES

1. Gently toss the oranges, pomelo, avocado, and almonds in a bowl.

2. Whisk together the poppy seeds, lemon juice, olive oil, honey, and salt and pepper to taste in a small bowl until it becomes emulsified. Toss the vinaigrette with the citrus salad.

3. Serve the citrus salad on a bed of lettuce.

SOUTHERN SIMPLE: Pomelo is in season during the winter months. These big citrus fruits resemble grapefruit and, like grapefruit, come in a variety of colors. Look for fruits that smell slightly sweet and seem heavy for their size.

SOUTHERN SIMPLE: If you would like to make this ahead, prepare all the fruits, but keep the avocado separate and add it to the dressing. The citrus juice in the dressing will keep the avocado from turning brown. Then toss the dressing and fruits together just before serving.

SOUTHERN SKINNY: This salad has a bit of protein to keep you going and fiber to fill you up.

APPLE-TOMATO SOUP

The Big Apple. To most people, this means New York City. But to me, Cornelia, Georgia, will always be the Big Apple. Right in the middle of my hometown, at the railroad depot, sits a bright-red replica of a North Georgia apple. The statue is fifteen feet tall and twenty-two feet around and serves as the centerpiece to the town's annual fall festival.

Georgia's Appalachian foothills area is known for its apples, which come to market in late August—a perfect time for making this soup! Summer's tomato season is winding down and apple-picking time begins.

Makes 4 servings

1 TABLESPOON OLIVE OIL

1 CUP DICED CELERY

1 CUP DICED CARROT

½ CUP DICED ONION

1 Golden Delicious APPLE, PEELED AND DICED

3 GARLIC CLOVES, MINCED

2 CUPS CHOPPED TOMATOES

1 CUP VEGETABLE BROTH

2 TEASPOONS APPLE CIDER VINEGAR

2 TABLESPOONS CHOPPED FRESH BASIL

½ CUP HEAVY (WHIPPING) CREAM

SALT AND FRESHLY GROUND BLACK PEPPER

GARNISH

¼ CUP CHOPPED TOMATOES

¼ CUP CHOPPED Golden Delicious APPLES

SEVERAL LEAVES FRESH BASIL

1. Heat the olive oil in a large saucepan or soup pot over medium heat. Add the celery, carrot, onion, and apple and cook, stirring, until softened, 3 to 5 minutes. Stir in the garlic and cook for 2 minutes. Add the tomatoes, vegetable broth, and vinegar. Bring to a boil, reduce the heat to low, and simmer for 20 to 25 minutes to thicken the soup. Stir in the basil and cream.

2. Puree in a stand blender or with a hand blender in the pot until smooth. Season with salt and pepper to taste.

3. Serve garnished with a bit of chopped tomatoes and apples. Top with fresh basil.

ASPARAGUS WRAPPED IN LEAVES

These are so nice for a springtime party. I like the nutty flavor of Asiago cheese and, as always, I add a kick—red pepper flakes do the trick here.

Don't be intimidated by working with phyllo dough! Just gather up some volunteers and form an assembly line—that's how we do it. Once you get the hang of it, it's quite rewarding to see and taste your work. I do have a couple of tips: turn off the ceiling fan in the kitchen and don't work around drafts. The circulating air will dry out the pastry pretty quickly and make it rip and crack. Also, make sure to let the pastry thaw in the refrigerator (I try to remember to take it from the freezer the day before). This helps keep condensation off the thin sheets; if allowed to thaw on the counter, the layers next to the packaging will be soggy.

Makes 6 servings

1 POUND ASPARAGUS SPEARS, TOUGH ENDS TRIMMED

ONE 1-POUND PACKAGE FROZEN PHYLLO DOUGH, THAWED

8 TABLESPOONS (1 STICK) BUTTER, MELTED

1 CUP GRATED ASIAGO CHEESE

RED PEPPER FLAKES

SALT

1. Preheat the oven to 400°F.

2. Bring a large pot of water to a boil and blanch the asparagus for about 3 minutes. Drain the asparagus spears and pat them dry.

3. Open the pastry sheets and work with one at a time. Keep the remaining dough covered. Cut a sheet in half with kitchen scissors. Brush one half-sheet with melted butter. Sprinkle 2 tablespoons Asiago and some pepper flakes on top. Lay an asparagus spear along the edge of the phyllo and roll it as tightly as possible, working gently and leaving the top of the spear exposed. Place on a rimmed baking sheet seam side down. Brush with a little more melted butter and season with salt. Repeat with the remaining ingredients.

4. Bake until golden brown, 7 to 10 minutes.

SOUTHERN SIMPLE: This crispy pastry-wrapped asparagus can be assembled, placed on a lined baking sheet, and wrapped tightly in plastic wrap. Store them in the refrigerator until ready to bake.

PEANUT BUTTER YOGURT DIP

This is one of my daughter's favorite concoctions to whip up in our stand mixer, which she calls the "Blister." It's sticky fun to do the measuring, and she gets a little practice in counting, too. Mama always said, "When you're cooking and measuring, always count out loud so you don't lose count." This is a great afternoon porch snack served with Strawberry Limeade (page 187). We serve this with apple slices, graham crackers, or pretzel sticks.

Makes about 2 cups

1½ CUPS PLAIN YOGURT

7 TABLESPOONS PEANUT BUTTER

3 TABLESPOONS HONEY

1 TABLESPOON NUTELLA (CHOCOLATE HAZELNUT SPREAD)

PINCH OF SALT

Using an electric mixer or by hand, blend all the ingredients together until smooth. Chill for at least 30 minutes. Serve with fresh apple slices, graham crackers, or pretzel sticks.

SOUTHERN MOTHER: Coat the interior of the measuring utensils and bowl with a quick shot of cooking spray so the sticky ingredients will release better.

PARMESAN BAKED TOMATOES

When summer is almost over and the tomatoes start to dwindle, I'll take the ones that are not good enough for slicing for sandwiches—but which are still pretty good—and bake them, simply seasoned with Parmesan and oregano.

Makes 4 servings

4 LARGE TOMATOES

1 TEASPOON SALT

¼ TEASPOON FRESHLY GROUND BLACK PEPPER

½ CUP GRATED PARMESAN CHEESE

¼ TEASPOON RED PEPPER FLAKES

2 TABLESPOONS CHOPPED FRESH OREGANO

1. Preheat the oven to 450°F.

2. Slice the tomatoes in half and place them cut side up in a baking dish. Season with the salt and pepper. Evenly sprinkle the Parmesan cheese, pepper flakes, and oregano on top. Bake until the Parmesan is beginning to brown and bubble, about 20 minutes.

SOUTHERN MOTHER: Daisy's friends like theirs a little more on the pizza-tasting side, so I'll top theirs with mozzarella.

SOUTHERN SKINNY: These roasted tomatoes are a flavorful addition to the morning when served up with an egg white omelet.

PEPPER JELLY–BUTTERED CORN SUMMER SPREAD

Such a summer delight! Sometimes I like nothing more for dinner than a big spread of vegetables—maybe some sliced tomatoes, butter beans, field peas with snaps, and of course, corn on the cob. My Daisy and I can put away some fresh corn! This corn cooks on a grill pan and then gets a spread of pepper jelly butter. The hot, sweet, buttery spread clings to the grilled corn and gives it a delightful glaze.

Makes 4 servings

8 TABLESPOONS (1 STICK) BUTTER, AT ROOM TEMPERATURE

3 TABLESPOONS PEPPER JELLY

1 TABLESPOON CHOPPED FRESH PARSLEY

4 EARS OF CORN, SHUCKED, SILK REMOVED, AND CUT IN HALF

OLIVE OIL, FOR BRUSHING

SALT AND FRESHLY GROUND BLACK PEPPER

1. Place a grill pan over medium-high heat or preheat a gas or charcoal grill.

2. Combine the butter, pepper jelly, and parsley in a small bowl and mix well.

3. Brush the corn with olive oil and season it liberally with salt and pepper. Grill the corn, turning often, until charred on all sides, about 8 minutes. Spread the butter mixture on the hot corn and serve at once.

SOUTHERN SIMPLE: One of my favorite varieties of corn is called Butter & Sugar. It's a beautiful bicolor, with both white and yellow kernels.

SOUTHERN MOTHER: If you hear a shriek when the kids are shucking and find a corn worm, tell them he did them a favor and picked the sweetest cob out for them!

GRILLED CREAMED CORN

If my sweetheart, Schlappy, has the grill fired up, I'll throw extra corn on the grill to have for later in the week. When it's cooked and cool enough to handle, I'll slice the kernels off the cob and stick them in the fridge. Then in a couple of days, I make this spicy creamed corn and have some of that backyard summer flavor when we're cooking indoors—away from mosquitoes.

Makes 6 servings

6 EARS OF CORN, SHUCKED, SILK REMOVED

3 TABLESPOONS UNSALTED BUTTER

2 JALAPEÑOS, SEEDED AND FINELY DICED

SALT AND FRESHLY GROUND BLACK PEPPER

1 TABLESPOON ALL-PURPOSE FLOUR

1 CUP HEAVY (WHIPPING) CREAM

¼ CUP GRATED PARMESAN CHEESE

2 TABLESPOONS CHOPPED FRESH PARSLEY

1. Place a grill pan over medium-high heat or preheat a gas or charcoal grill. Grill the corn, turning occasionally, until tender and charred, 10 to 12 minutes.

2. When the corn is cool enough to handle, cut the kernels off the cob.

3. Heat the butter in a skillet over medium-high heat. Add the jalapeños and cook for 2 minutes. Add the corn and season with salt and pepper to taste. Cook until softened, about 3 minutes. Stir in the flour and cook for 1 minute. Reduce the heat to medium and add the cream. Simmer until the mixture thickens, 2 to 3 minutes.

4. Transfer half the mixture to a food processor and blend until smooth. Pour the pureed mixture back into the skillet and add the Parmesan and parsley. Cook over low heat until warmed through. Season with salt and pepper to taste. Serve warm.

SOUTHERN SIMPLE: Throw your jalapeños on the grill to get a bit of char before they're chopped, seeded, and added to the corn.

SOUTHERN MOTHER: Get the kids involved in shucking. I also like a gadget called a Corn Zipper; it makes short work of cutting the corn from the cob and directs it right into your bowl.

Sweet Potato Oven Fries with Berry Spicy Ketchup

I do love a rainy night, bundled up on the couch with my hubby and daughter. A movie and some sweet and salty snack—that's a perfect night. Even if we can all recite the words and songs to all the "princess films," it's still fun to giggle and sing along.

One of my favorite movie-night snacks is these baked fries, served along with a double-feature ketchup with berry-sweet tartness and chipotle heat.

Makes 4 servings

3 LARGE SWEET POTATOES, UNPEELED, CUT INTO WEDGES
2 TABLESPOONS CHOPPED FRESH PARSLEY
2 TABLESPOONS OLIVE OIL
SALT AND FRESHLY GROUND BLACK PEPPER
1 PINT RASPBERRIES
1 CUP KETCHUP
¼ CUP TABASCO CHIPOTLE PEPPER SAUCE

1. Preheat the oven to 375°F. Line a baking sheet with foil.

2. Combine the sweet potato wedges, parsley, olive oil, and salt and pepper to taste in a large bowl. Toss well to coat the potatoes evenly. Spread them out on the lined baking sheet and bake until crispy and golden brown, 20 to 25 minutes.

3. Meanwhile, puree the raspberries in a blender. Pass the puree through a fine-mesh sieve over a bowl (discard the seeds). Add the ketchup and chipotle sauce to the bowl and mix well. Season with salt to taste.

4. Serve the fries hot with little dishes of the ketchup on the side.

SOUTHERN SIMPLE: This ketchup wakes up grilled salmon or chicken sandwiches, too.

SOUTHERN SIMPLE: For a fun twist, try purple sweet potatoes or a mixture of white, orange, and purple.

SOUTHERN MOTHER: I dream of being the voice of an animated movie character one day. I would love to sing as a princess, but I'll take anything they offer me!

The fries are pictured on page 175.

BUTTERMILK MASHED POTATOES

Whether it's served with Country-Fried Steak (page 37) or Sunday Pot Roast (page 127), this golden, garlic-and-chive-flecked mashed potato recipe—with a buttermilk tang—is going to be served at our house. These are wonderful on their own but stupendous as a boat for gravy.

Makes 4 servings

2 POUNDS YUKON GOLD POTATOES, PEELED AND CUT INTO CHUNKS

¼ CUP MILK

½ CUP BUTTERMILK

1 GARLIC CLOVE, MINCED

4 TABLESPOONS (½ STICK) BUTTER

2 TABLESPOONS CHOPPED FRESH CHIVES

1 TEASPOON SALT

¼ TEASPOON FRESHLY GROUND BLACK PEPPER

1. Place the potatoes in a pot with cold, salted water to cover. Bring the water to a boil over medium-high heat, turn the heat to medium-low, and simmer, uncovered, until the potatoes fall apart easily when pierced with a fork, 10 to 15 minutes.

2. Meanwhile, heat the milk, buttermilk, garlic, and butter in a small saucepan over low heat. Make sure it doesn't boil. Keep the liquid warm until the potatoes are done.

3. Drain the potatoes in a colander, then transfer them to a large bowl. Using an electric mixer, whip the potatoes while slowly pouring in the hot buttermilk mixture. Add enough of the mixture to make the potatoes creamy. You may need more or less buttermilk depending how dry or wet the potatoes are. Mix in the chives, salt, and pepper and serve.

> **SOUTHERN SIMPLE:** If you're not in the habit of keeping buttermilk, grab some powdered buttermilk from your grocery's baking section and you'll always have some on hand.

> **SOUTHERN MOTHER:** One cup of just about any vegetable puree can be folded into the potatoes; try cauliflower, carrots, or green peas.

HOMEMADE TOMATO SAUCE

My family is fond of pasta. We like all the varieties—from curly to straight. With our hectic schedules, when I do find time to make good homemade tomato sauce, I tend make a big batch. We'll usually have some for dinner that night, and then I put up some in the freezer. That way, on those hectic nights, I can heat the sauce, and by the time the pasta is ready, dinner is done!

Makes 6 cups

½ CUP OLIVE OIL

1 SMALL VIDALIA ONION, FINELY CHOPPED

5 GARLIC CLOVES, MINCED

1 LARGE CARROT, GRATED

TWO 28-OUNCE CANS WHOLE PEELED TOMATOES

1 BAY LEAF

2 TABLESPOONS CHOPPED FRESH BASIL

SALT AND FRESHLY GROUND BLACK PEPPER

Heat the olive oil in a Dutch oven over medium heat. Add the onion and cook until softened, about 5 minutes. Add the garlic and carrot and cook for 5 minutes. Hand-crush the tomatoes as you add them to the pot, then add the can juices, bay leaf, and basil. Bring the mixture to a boil, then reduce the heat to medium-low and let the sauce simmer for an hour or so to thicken. Season with salt and pepper to taste.

SOUTHERN SIMPLE: This is a great base for many other dishes: spaghetti and meatballs, lasagna, Bolognese, and so on.

The carrot and Vidalia onion add a bit of sweetness to the sauce.

SOUTHERN MOTHER: An English muffin topped with this sauce and cheese makes a quick mini-pizza snack.

DONNA'S SPAGHETTI CASSEROLE WITH FENNEL

There's that flavor to Italian sausage that everybody loves. I think it's the fennel seed. We often try to do a "Meatless Monday" meal, and my mother-in-law, Donna, shared this recipe with me. The fresh fennel in this quick-to-assemble casserole adds an intriguing flavor that keeps it from falling flat. When the fennel bakes down with the mushrooms, they taste like Italian sausage. If you don't bring it up, no one's the wiser that it was even Meatless Monday. Shhhh!

Makes one 2-quart casserole

COOKING SPRAY

2 TABLESPOONS OLIVE OIL

1 CUP THINLY SLICED ONION

3 GARLIC CLOVES, MINCED

2 CUPS SLICED BUTTON MUSHROOMS

1 CUP THINLY SLICED FENNEL

3 CUPS HOMEMADE TOMATO SAUCE (PAGE 159) OR STORE-BOUGHT PASTA SAUCE

1 POUND SPAGHETTI, BROKEN INTO 2-INCH PIECES, COOKED

1 CUP SHREDDED MOZZARELLA CHEESE

1 CUP SHREDDED PARMESAN CHEESE

2 TABLESPOONS CHOPPED FRESH PARSLEY

1. Preheat the oven to 400°F. Coat a 2-quart baking dish with cooking spray.

2. Heat the olive oil in a Dutch oven over medium heat. Add the onion and cook until softened, about 5 minutes. Add the garlic and cook for 2 minutes. Add the mushrooms and fennel and cook until the vegetables are soft, about 7 minutes. Add the tomato sauce and cooked spaghetti and mix well. Salt to taste.

3. Pour the mixture into the baking dish. Top the casserole with the mozzarella, Parmesan, and parsley. Bake until the cheese is golden brown, 12 to 15 minutes.

SOUTHERN SIMPLE: This casserole freezes well. It's a great one to double—one for dinner and one for stashing away or sharing.

SOUTHERN SKINNY: Sometimes less really is more—try skipping the mozzarella and using only the Parmesan. You'll get a satisfyingly cheesy flavor and save a couple of grams of fat.

CREAMY SMOKED MAC AND CHEESE

A toasty garlic-crumb topping and a whiff of smoke really make this stovetop macaroni and cheese fit for grown folks. Let's face it: there is a lot of sad macaroni and cheese in the world. This recipe, however, elevates the humble dish. Think of all the possible ingredients you can include—even cooked crab or lobster if you want to start at the top!

Makes 6 servings

5 TABLESPOONS BUTTER

3 GARLIC CLOVES, MINCED

1 CUP PANKO BREADCRUMBS

¼ CUP GRATED PARMESAN CHEESE

1 TABLESPOON CHOPPED FRESH PARSLEY

1 POUND SPIRAL PASTA

¼ CUP ALL-PURPOSE FLOUR

1½ CUPS MILK

1 CUP HEAVY (WHIPPING) CREAM

1 TABLESPOON GARLIC POWDER

1 POUND SMOKED CHEDDAR OR GOUDA CHEESE, GRATED

SALT AND FRESHLY GROUND BLACK PEPPER

1. Melt 1 tablespoon of the butter in a skillet over low heat. Add the garlic and cook until it becomes fragrant, about 1 minute. Add the panko and toast until golden brown. Pour the breadcrumb mixture into a bowl, add the Parmesan and parsley, and stir to combine.

2. In a large pot of boiling salted water, cook the pasta al dente.

3. Meanwhile, melt the remaining 4 tablespoons butter in a large saucepan over medium-low heat. Add the flour and whisk until it starts to foam, about 2 minutes. Slowly add the milk, heavy cream, and garlic powder, whisking constantly. Keep whisking until the sauce thickens, taking care not to let it boil. Add the cheese in small batches, whisking after each until the cheese is melted. Season with salt and pepper to taste.

4. Drain the cooked pasta. Toss the pasta and cheese sauce together and stir to mix well. Serve in bowls and top with toasted breadcrumbs.

SOUTHERN SIMPLE: If you don't have any smoked cheese, the slightest drop of natural liquid smoke flavoring can be added to the cheese sauce.

Josh's Chicken Alfredo

My brother, Josh, is a hardworking, tenderhearted country boy who is incredibly gifted in the kitchen. He's so passionate about cooking and has such a knack for throwing something amazing together. One of these days I just know he's going to have his own very successful restaurant. He and I love to cook together. With the miles between us, we're always texting and sending pictures of what we're cooking. With just a photo, he can make me homesick and hungry all at once! And, well, Josh really scored when he married his darling wife, Jade. They both admit that his take on Alfredo helped win her heart. He seasons chicken thighs and bakes them in the oven while preparing the beautiful mushroom cream sauce. Combined with bow-tie pasta and a sprinkle of grated cheese, it is no wonder this recipe wooed sweet Jade.

Makes 4 servings

1½ POUNDS BONELESS, SKINLESS CHICKEN THIGHS

1 TEASPOON GARLIC POWDER

1 TEASPOON ONION POWDER

1 TEASPOON PAPRIKA

SALT AND FRESHLY GROUND BLACK PEPPER

3 TABLESPOONS BUTTER

2 TABLESPOONS OLIVE OIL

8 OUNCES CREMINI (BABY BELLA) MUSHROOMS, SLICED

2 GARLIC CLOVES, MINCED

1 CUP HEAVY (WHIPPING) CREAM

1 CUP MILK

1½ CUPS SHREDDED ITALIAN CHEESE BLEND

1 CUP SHREDDED MILD CHEDDAR CHEESE

10 OUNCES BOW-TIE PASTA

1. Preheat the oven to 400°F.

2. Season the chicken thighs on both sides with the garlic powder, onion powder, paprika, 1 teaspoon salt, and ½ teaspoon pepper. Place them on a baking sheet and bake until cooked through, 20 to 25 minutes.

3. Heat the butter and olive oil in a skillet over medium heat. Add the mushrooms and cook until tender, about 5 minutes. Add the garlic and cook for 1 minute, or until fragrant. Stir in the cream and milk. When the milk is hot, slowly add the

cheeses and continue to stir until the cheese melts and is smooth and creamy. Season with salt and pepper to taste. Keep warm until serving.

4. In a large pot of boiling salted water, cook the pasta until al dente. Drain and toss the pasta with the cheese sauce. Stir well. Serve the chicken on top of the pasta.

The vase in this photo is one of my daddy's first pieces of pottery. It's an absolute treasure to me.

CHICKEN AND HASH BROWN CASSEROLE

Sometimes you have to multitask. When one of those days rolls around, the kind where there seems to be too many irons in the fire—and a few fires to put out—I'll turn to this casserole. I can snatch chicken and hash browns from the freezer and whip this up in no time flat.

Makes 6 servings

ONE 2-POUND PACKAGE FROZEN DICED HASH BROWN POTATOES, THAWED

1 CUP DICED ONION

TWO 10.75-OUNCE CANS CONDENSED CREAM OF CHICKEN SOUP

8 TABLESPOONS (1 STICK) BUTTER, MELTED

1½ CUPS GRATED CHEDDAR CHEESE

3 CUPS DICED COOKED CHICKEN

1 TEASPOON SALT

½ TEASPOON FRESHLY GROUND BLACK PEPPER

1 TABLESPOON CHOPPED FRESH PARSLEY

1. Preheat the oven to 350°F.

2. Combine the ingredients in a large bowl, mix well, and spread the mixture evenly in a greased 9 x 13-inch baking dish. Bake until golden brown, about 1 hour.

Mama's Chicken Biscuit Pie

This savory chicken cobbler has a fluffy golden biscuit topping. I love serving this dish to the family. It is just homey goodness, like a big biscuit comforter spread over a bed of vegetables and tender chicken—all wrapped up in a golden cream sauce!

Makes 6 servings

BISCUIT TOPPING

1 CUP SELF-RISING FLOUR

8 TABLESPOONS (1 STICK) BUTTER

½ TEASPOON SALT

¼ TEASPOON FRESHLY GROUND BLACK PEPPER

1 CUP MILK

FILLING

2 TABLESPOONS SALTED BUTTER

2 HEAPING TABLESPOONS ALL-PURPOSE FLOUR

1 CUP HEAVY (WHIPPING) CREAM

1½ CUPS CHICKEN BROTH

½ TEASPOON CHICKEN BASE

SALT AND FRESHLY GROUND BLACK PEPPER

½ CUP FINELY DICED ONION

½ CUP FINELY DICED CARROT

¼ CUP FROZEN GREEN PEAS

1 JALAPEÑO, SEEDED AND FINELY DICED

1 BONELESS, SKINLESS CHICKEN BREAST, COOKED AND CUT INTO SMALL PIECES (ABOUT 1½ CUPS)

1. Preheat the oven to 350°F.

2. Make the biscuit topping: Using a pastry blender or two table knives, cut the flour, butter, salt, and pepper together in a medium bowl until the consistency of crumbs. Add the milk and stir just until combined. The dough will be on the wet side. Set aside.

3. Make the filling: Melt the butter in a large saucepan over medium-low heat. Add the flour and whisk until it becomes a smooth, thick paste. Cook until barely golden, 2 to 3 minutes. Whisk in the cream and chicken stock and cook, continuing to whisk, until the mixture begins to thicken, like a gravy. Add the chicken base and

stir. Season with salt and pepper to taste. Add the onion, carrot, peas, jalapeño, and chicken and mix well.

4. Pour the mixture into the pie pan. Using a large spoon, drop the dough on top of the filling to create the biscuit topping. It doesn't have to be perfect, but make sure to cover the entire surface with the dough pieces.

5. Bake the pie until the biscuit topping is golden brown, 45 to 50 minutes. Let it sit for 15 minutes before serving.

SOUTHERN MOTHER: When someone has a baby, after the initial flurry of guests—about three weeks in—my mother will drop by the new parents' home with this fluffy biscuit-topped treat. Her timing for this lovely gesture is usually spot-on.

Happy, Happy Grilled Turkey Burgers with Maple Caramelized Onions

My husband, Steve, is a lover of all things outdoors. He has a green thumb and will literally save trees and baby them at the seedling stage. He spots them like four-leaf clovers in the yard and marks them so they don't get mowed down. He also loves a backyard cookout.

This recipe works well for us because these lean turkey burgers don't bust my nutrition goals for the family, so I'm happy, and the intensely deep sweetness of the dark, caramelized onions keep Steve from missing a great burger experience, so he's happy.

Makes 4 servings

CARAMELIZED ONIONS

2 LARGE VIDALIA ONIONS, THINLY SLICED

3 TABLESPOONS MAPLE SYRUP

¼ TEASPOON CAYENNE PEPPER

SALT AND FRESHLY GROUND BLACK PEPPER

BURGERS

1½ POUNDS LEAN GROUND TURKEY

1 TABLESPOON WHOLE-GRAIN MUSTARD

3 GARLIC CLOVES, MINCED

1 EGG

2 TABLESPOONS CHOPPED FRESH PARSLEY

½ TEASPOON SALT

¼ TEASPOON FRESHLY GROUND BLACK PEPPER

OLIVE OIL, FOR BRUSHING

4 BURGER-SIZE CHEDDAR CHEESE SLICES

4 SESAME SEED BUNS, SPLIT AND TOASTED

1. Make the caramelized onions: Cook the onions in a large skillet over low heat, stirring often, until they begin to caramelize and turn brown, 20 to 25 minutes. Add the maple syrup and cayenne and season with salt and black pepper to taste. Cook until the onions are caramelized, another 7 to 8 minutes.

2. Place a grill pan over medium-high heat or preheat a gas or charcoal grill.

(continued)

3. Make the burgers: Mix the ground turkey, mustard, garlic, egg, parsley, salt, and pepper in a large bowl. Form the mixture into four 6-ounce patties. Brush each side with olive oil and season with salt and pepper.

4. Grill the turkey burgers for 12 to 15 minutes total, flipping the burgers once. Place a slice of cheese on each burger, top with caramelized onions, and serve on toasted sesame seed buns.

SOUTHERN SIMPLE: These sweet onions are a great accompaniment to roasted pork or wild game. If you make a double batch of the onions, half can be saved in the refrigerator for up to a month. They're a fantastic addition to grilled cheese sandwiches, too.

SOUTHERN SIMPLE: I often serve these burgers with Sweet Potato Oven Fries with Berry Spicy Ketchup (page 157).

SOUTHERN SKINNY: Some ground turkey can actually contain more fat than ground beef. Look for ground turkey labeled 90/10; this means it is 90 percent lean ground meat and 10 percent fat.

Vidalia onions come from one specific region of my home state of Georgia that has low-sulfur soil. Each spring the town of Vidalia hosts a festival celebrating the official state vegetable. There is even a Little Miss Vidalia Onion pageant!

RUBBED RIB-EYE STEAK

I get my curious streak from my daddy. I wanted to know more about butchering, so I be-bopped up into Porter Road Butcher, a local Nashville butcher shop, to learn all about it. Those fellows handed me the biggest knife I've ever held, called a scimitar. But I wrapped my apron around my waist, and the guys gave me a lesson in Butchering 101. Might be best for me to stick to singing, though!

The rib-eye is one of the most flavorful cuts of steak. Meat from the rib section is more tender and has more marbling. Get to know your butcher; you can learn a whole bunch from him!

Makes 4 servings

3 TABLESPOONS DARK-ROAST COFFEE BEANS

2 TEASPOONS RED PEPPER FLAKES

1 TEASPOON CUMIN SEEDS

1 TEASPOON MUSTARD SEEDS

1 TEASPOON FENNEL SEEDS

2 TEASPOONS SMOKED PAPRIKA

1 TABLESPOON DARK BROWN SUGAR

1 TEASPOON FRESHLY GROUND BLACK PEPPER

FOUR 6- TO 8-OUNCE RIB-EYE STEAKS, 1 INCH THICK

OLIVE OIL, FOR THE GRILL

1 TABLESPOON SALT

1. Place the coffee beans and all the spices except the salt in a spice grinder and pulverize until finely crushed.

2. Rub the spice mixture all over the steaks. Cover them with plastic wrap and refrigerate for at least 30 minutes to overnight. Bring the steaks to room temperature before grilling.

3. Preheat a gas or charcoal grill to medium. Brush olive oil on the grill rack so the steaks won't stick. Season the steaks with the salt and grill for 4 to 5 minutes on each side or until the desired doneness. Let the meat rest off the heat for 5 minutes before serving.

SOUTHERN SIMPLE: Season the rib-eye steaks with all the spices, but hold off on the salt until you're ready to cook. Salt will draw out moisture. This is a good general rule for grilling.

Use any cut of meat with this spice rub. Always allow your meat to come to room temperature before cooking to ensure even cooking. And remember to let meat rest after cooking!

*Rubbed Rib-Eye Steak and Sweet Potato Oven Fries
with Berry Spicy Ketchup, page 157*

ROASTED FIGS WITH GOAT CHEESE AND VANILLA HONEY

One whole side of the house where I grew up is covered by a gigantic fig tree. Actually, we had two huge fig trees. I used to impatiently await late summer so we could pick and eat those delicious figs right off the tree. I loved sneaking up under their broad, shady leaves to pluck sweet figs off the branches and pop them in my mouth. I'd be so proud of myself for beating the birds to them. We'd have to fight off the yellow jackets because I guess they loved those figs as much as we did—but it was always worth the risk of a sting. When we moved into our home in Nashville, Schlappy got a fig tree for me. It was one of the sweetest gifts I've ever been given because he knows how very special those trees are to me. Schlappy planted mine on the side of our house, too, and I hope to see it grow as strong as my love for that man.

Makes 12 stuffed figs

12 FRESH FIGS

2 OUNCES GOAT CHEESE

¼ CUP HONEY

1 VANILLA BEAN, SPLIT LENGTHWISE

¼ CUP CHOPPED PECANS

1. Preheat the oven to 425°F. Line a rimmed baking sheet with parchment paper.

2. Slice an X through the stem end of each fig, cutting only three-quarters of the way down, so they are still left whole. Stuff the figs with goat cheese. Place them on the baking sheet and bake until the figs are softened and the cheese has just started to melt, about 12 minutes.

3. Meanwhile, warm the honey in a small saucepan over low heat. Scrape the vanilla seeds into the honey and stir to combine.

4. Serve the figs drizzled with the warm vanilla honey and garnished with chopped pecans.

SOUTHERN SIMPLE: Pitted plums are also wonderful when roasted the same way as the figs.

SOUTHERN MOTHER: If you have a healthy fig tree, it's easy to share cuttings. To propagate a fig tree, simply bury a lower branch beneath the soil and cover with some straw or hay. Next year, when you uncover the branch you'll find that roots have begun to grow. A fig tree is such a wonderful housewarming present.

Sweet Orange Rolls

I make these ooey-gooey, cinnamony, orange-iced sweet rolls the day after we go out for pizza. (I'm lucky to have a great local pizza parlor nearby.) When we go there for dinner, on the way out I ask if I can buy two pizzas' worth of dough. I put it away in the refrigerator first thing when we get home. The next morning, I give Daisy one ball of dough to play with while I set to making these buttery, orange-scented rolls.

Makes 10 sweet rolls

1 BALL STORE-BOUGHT PIZZA DOUGH

6 TABLESPOONS BUTTER, MELTED

½ CUP TURBINADO SUGAR

½ CUP PACKED BROWN SUGAR

1 TABLESPOON GROUND CINNAMON

⅛ TEASPOON SALT

2 CUPS POWDERED SUGAR

GRATED ZEST OF 2 ORANGES

2 TABLESPOONS PLUS 1 TEASPOON FRESH ORANGE JUICE

1. Preheat the oven to 375°F. Grease and flour an 8-inch round cake pan.

2. Sprinkle some flour on a clean surface. Roll out the pizza dough to a rectangle ⅛-inch thick and about 20 inches wide.

3. Brush the dough with 3 tablespoons of the melted butter. Mix the turbinado sugar, brown sugar, cinnamon, and salt in a small bowl. Sprinkle the mixture evenly over the dough, then drizzle the remaining melted butter on top. Starting on the side closest to you, roll the dough into a cylinder. Cut the cylinder crosswise into 2-inch-wide slices.

4. Fill the baking dish with the rolls, cut side up, allowing the rolls to touch. Bake until golden brown, about 30 minutes. Cool the rolls completely in the pan.

5. Meanwhile, whisk together the powdered sugar, orange zest, and orange juice in a medium bowl until smooth. Drizzle the orange glaze over the warm orange rolls.

SOUTHERN SIMPLE: Look for frozen or refrigerated pizza dough at your grocery.

TRIED-AND-TRUE ALMOND POUND CAKE

My grandmother Burrell has shared this recipe with me and countless others who've inquired over the years. The unique part of the recipe is that the baking is started in a cold oven. The recipe for this golden, tender pound cake is a wonderful addition to a wedding shower gift of a nice Bundt cake pan. It's a gift a couple will enjoy for a lifetime.

Makes 1 Bundt cake

COOKING SPRAY

2 STICKS (½ POUND) BUTTER, AT ROOM TEMPERATURE

½ CUP VEGETABLE SHORTENING

3 CUPS SUGAR

6 EGGS, AT ROOM TEMPERATURE

3 CUPS ALL-PURPOSE FLOUR, SIFTED 3 TIMES (SEE SOUTHERN MOTHER)

½ TEASPOON SALT

½ TEASPOON BAKING POWDER

1 CUP SOUR CREAM

4 TEASPOONS ALMOND EXTRACT

1. Coat a Bundt pan with cooking spray.

2. Using an electric mixer, cream the butter, shortening, and sugar in a large bowl until light and fluffy. Add the eggs one at a time, mixing well after each addition.

3. Sift the flour, salt, and baking powder together into a bowl.

4. Add the sour cream, almond extract, and flour mixture to the butter-sugar mixture and mix until just blended.

5. Pour the batter into the Bundt pan and place it in a cold oven. Turn the oven to 300°F and bake until a toothpick inserted in the center comes out clean and the top springs back slightly when touched, about 1 hour and 20 to 25 minutes. Cool the cake in the pan, then unmold it onto a serving plate or cake stand.

SOUTHERN SIMPLE: This cake does not use a lot of baking powder. Instead, the large amount of eggs helps this rich pound cake rise.

SOUTHERN MOTHER: The flour in this recipe is sifted three times. I like to do it over a sheet of parchment paper with a large bowl handy to catch the flour between sifts. It's a fun job for the children, but be sure to measure again because a good deal of it might end up on the floor!

One of my sweetest memories is of my family's Christmas baking tradition. I'd always mark it on my December calendar early in the year. My grandmother would open up her kitchen to my mama, sister, nieces, cousins, and me. We were each given our own jobs and would bake all day long—measuring, rolling out little balls, dipping chocolate, and—of course—*tasting* . . . till we had tummy aches. To this day, I love hosting this traditional day of baking with all the lovely ladies—little and big—in our sweet family.

Black Walnut Cake

I married my first husband, Steve Roads, young, at just age twenty-one. We thought we were going to grow old together. I saw us walking the road of life side by side. Then, in an instant, my husband was gone. He had a heart attack and died. I was devastated. I felt overwhelming pain, a crushing rawness I hope never to experience again.

After we laid him to rest up in our family cemetery plot in Georgia, I returned to Nashville.

I was consumed by all the things that come along with the tremendous shock of losing a loved one so suddenly. The initial days were a blur; a sense of the unimaginable hung around, followed by the burden of duties to tend to, then the stark, quiet pall of grief. During this time the sight of food turned my stomach. Everyone was trying to feed me, but I was unable to eat. Friends and neighbors had brought so much food to the house that one neighbor brought over a little refrigerator to hold the excess. But I could not eat. The first few days, I would force myself to get up and eat just a chicken leg a day—but that was all I could force down. I was sick with grief.

On one of the first few days back home alone, I remember my friend Lisa's mother, Mrs. Jones, came to the door like an angel and brought me a beautiful, lovely black walnut cake. She offered it so sweetly, with just a minute's visit.

*I took that cake into the quiet kitchen and set it down. I was home with just my dog, Buck, and I thought—and maybe even said to Buck—*You know what? I need to eat something.* So I cut me a piece of that cake and set it on a little dish and got me a fork. That cake was incredible: perfectly done, with cream cheese icing and just the right amount of sweet. It was late morning. Then, later in the day, I thought,* You know what? I'm going to have me another piece of that cake. *I went on like that for several days—maybe four or five—taking the cake out of the small refrigerator, unwrapping it, cutting a slice, rewrapping it, and returning it to the small refrigerator when I felt I could handle the least little bite of something.*

When the cake was gone I was by no means done with my grief, but I'd regained some of my strength and my appetite. Mrs. Jones gave me such a generous gift of her time. You see, a lot goes into making a black walnut cake. Her homemade condolence truly comforted me. I look back on that time with such sadness, but in the midst of that sadness, there are gems of kindness. I have never—and will never—forget the gift of that black walnut cake. I thank Mrs. Jones for it each time I see her. When I think back on that time and the kindness shown to me, it helps temper the sadness even today.

(continued)

CAKE

8 TABLESPOONS (1 STICK) BUTTER, AT ROOM TEMPERATURE

½ CUP VEGETABLE SHORTENING

2 CUPS GRANULATED SUGAR

4 LARGE EGGS

3½ CUPS ALL-PURPOSE FLOUR

2 TEASPOONS BAKING SODA

½ TEASPOON SALT

1½ CUPS BUTTERMILK

2 TEASPOONS VANILLA EXTRACT

1½ CUPS GROUND BLACK WALNUTS

FROSTING

16 OUNCES CREAM CHEESE, AT ROOM TEMPERATURE

2 STICKS (½ POUND) BUTTER, AT ROOM TEMPERATURE

8 CUPS POWDERED SUGAR, SIFTED

1 TABLESPOON VANILLA EXTRACT

1. Make the cake: Preheat the oven to 350°F. Grease three 9-inch round cake pans.

2. Using an electric mixer, cream the butter, shortening, and granulated sugar in a large bowl. Add the eggs one at a time, beating well after each addition. In a separate bowl, combine the flour, baking soda, and salt. Add to the creamed butter alternately with the buttermilk, mixing well after each addition. Then stir in the vanilla, followed by the ground walnuts.

3. Evenly divide the batter among the 3 cake pans. Bake until a toothpick inserted in the center of a cake comes out clean, about 25 minutes. Cool the cake layers thoroughly in the pans, then turn them out onto cooling racks.

4. Meanwhile, make the frosting: Using an electric mixer, beat the cream cheese in a large bowl until creamy and smooth. Beat in the butter. Slowly beat in the powdered sugar, then the vanilla.

5. Lay the bottom layer on a serving plate or cake stand. Frost the top of the layer. Top with the middle layer and frost it, then the top layer. Frost the top of the cake, then the sides.

SOUTHERN SIMPLE: Eastern black walnuts are like hardheaded cousins of the familiar English walnut. They are so difficult to crack that most times a hammer has to be employed. After a long process of gathering, hulling, curing, and cracking, aside from a meager yield of nutmeats, you end up with hands stained like a sepia-toned photo. Thankfully, good-quality black walnuts can easily be procured online from Hammons Products (www.hammonsproducts.com). Still, keep an eye out for this vanishing crop at farmers' markets and if you see a fellow selling them out of a truck bed, be sure to pick some up.

When Schlappy and I met, he was the stage manager for one of our first tours. He and I were good friends. I remember that our bunks were near each other on the bus. He was so kind and respectful and knew how much in love I was with my husband. There was never a romantic thought between the two of us. His dad passed away soon after that tour, and he moved back to Virginia to help out his mother while pursuing his master's degree in business. Schlappy called me one day after Steve died, not knowing of his death. He wanted to come see us at a show we were booked for in his hometown of Lynchburg, Virginia. Of course I filled him in on what had happened.

Long story short, he started calling me often to check on me, just as so many of my other friends did. But *he* never stopped calling! He was so easy to talk to about my grief, as he had recently lost his best friend. He pulled me out of the deepest, most painful hole imaginable and showed me that I could love again. He fixed me. He gave up his own career in Virginia to come on the road to sell our T-shirts so that we could be together. He rescued me from fear and loneliness—and made me laugh again. On our honeymoon, I tucked away a little souvenir in my tummy, and nine months later our Daisy was born. It was like a wedding gift straight from heaven. Never had I ever wanted anything more than to be a mommy! Now, *that's* a second chance! He's a wonderful father and can do, make, or fix *anything*! And, more important, he eats dessert first!

STRAWBERRY LIMEADE

I brake in an instant to go to a tag sale, an estate sale, or an auction. At our wonderful Nashville flea market, I picked up a terrific juicer. It's the kind with a big handle to crank down and squeeze fresh citrus. Its acquisition has led to many experiments with "ades" of all sorts. This is one of our favorites, a combination of bright strawberry and zingy lime.

Makes about 8 cups

1 CUP SUGAR

1 CUP FRESH LIME JUICE

1 CUP FROZEN SWEETENED STRAWBERRIES, THAWED AND PUREED

LIME WEDGES, FOR GARNISH

1. Combine the sugar and 1 cup water in a small saucepan. Bring to a boil over medium-low heat, stirring until the sugar is dissolved. Remove the simple syrup from the heat.

2. Pour the lime juice and pureed strawberries into a half-gallon jar. Add the simple syrup and 4 cups cold water. Stir and chill. Serve with lime wedges.

CHAPTER 5

Away

So much of my life has been spent on the road singing for my supper. I average about 200 days a year out on the road with Little Big Town, and much of the time we all have our families in tow. Three couples, three children, nannies, a band, and crew. We're quite the traveling circus at times. Generally, our schedule runs as follows: getting on the tour bus around midnight on Wednesday, then riding throughout the night to arrive in the city where we will perform on Thursday. Some mornings are spent doing interviews with local radio or television stations, often bringing our children. I find time to school Daisy and, if possible, we take the kids for an outing at a local museum or on a trip to the zoo. If we have some downtime, Karen and I will hit the flea markets or antique shops, since we're both dedicated pickers! We've found many treasured little dishes and tchotchkes on those hunts, and Karen seems to always find a good fur! In the afternoon we have sound check and then dinner. After that it's time to get all gussied up. We have a meet and greet, because we always love seeing and catching up with the good folks who buy our records and allow us to do what we love to do.

Then it's time to put on a show! After all these years, each show is still so exciting, all that welling up of energy and striving to make the connection with the audience. It's like Loretta Lynn said, "You have got to continue to grow or you're just like last night's cornbread. Stale and dry." After the show we might have a little gathering with radio or label execs, then it's back on the bus. We hop in our bunks and hopefully sleep as we roll through the night to the next town. Usually we're back home in Nashville by morning on Sunday—sometimes in time for church.

Years ago, I was feeling so intensely overwhelmed by the constant momentum of traveling that my dear husband, Schlappy, took my hand, looked me deep in my eyes, and said, "Wherever we are together, that is home." I took a deep breath, and then knew everything was okay. So these days, I'm down home all over the world!

PINEAPPLE CASSEROLE

Ready, set, go! I can practically assemble this casserole, bake it, and have it out the door a half hour from the time I walk into the kitchen. Sharp Cheddar and sweet pineapple get a buttery crumb topping here, and as it bakes, the pineapple juice thickens and absorbs some of the salty cracker crumbs. This is, as they say, more than the sum of its parts. I always like to have a few homemade dishes when we are out on the road, and this one is so quick to assemble and great for travel because it doesn't slosh around. It also doesn't really need to be served piping hot.

Makes 6 servings

¾ CUP SUGAR

5 HEAPING TABLESPOONS SELF-RISING FLOUR

TWO 15.25-OUNCE CANS PINEAPPLE TIDBITS, DRAINED

1½ CUPS GRATED CHEDDAR CHEESE

1 CUP RITZ CRACKER CRUMBS (FROM 1 SLEEVE, ABOUT 31 CRACKERS)

8 TABLESPOONS (1 STICK) BUTTER, MELTED

1. Preheat the oven to 375°F. Grease a 9 x 13-inch baking dish.

2. Combine the sugar and flour in a large bowl. Add the pineapple and mix to coat it well. Spread the mixture evenly in the baking dish and sprinkle the Cheddar over the top.

3. Mix together the cracker crumbs and melted butter in a medium bowl. Sprinkle the cracker mixture over the top of the casserole. Bake until golden brown, 25 to 30 minutes.

SOUTHERN SIMPLE: Canned apricots are a scrumptious substitute for pineapple in this casserole.

KALE SALAD WITH DATES

Schlappy's sweet sister, Michele, and her husband, Dave, live with their four adorable sons out in sunny Ventura, California, just a few blocks from the beach where Schlappy asked me to marry him. In fact, we got to share our exciting news with them first! It's always a treat to spend time with them when we visit the Golden State, and they're definitely my inspiration for this yummy salad. While touring we got a chance to do some visiting with them last summer, and I went kale crazy. I've always loved dates, so I thought a marriage of the two was in order. Dates thrive in the dry climate of Southern California, and kale is also grown in great abundance in the San Joaquin Valley. Upon returning home, I came up with this nutritious salad. It kinda makes me feel like a beach babe!

Makes 4 servings

1 POUND KALE, STEMMED AND CHOPPED, OR ONE 16-OUNCE BAG CHOPPED KALE

JUICE OF 1 LEMON

1¼ TEASPOONS KOSHER SALT

2 TABLESPOONS HONEY

½ TEASPOON RED PEPPER FLAKES

¼ CUP EXTRA-VIRGIN OLIVE OIL

½ SHALLOT, MINCED

¼ CUP CHOPPED PECANS OR PECAN PIECES

5 DATES, PITTED AND CHOPPED

1 LARGE HONEYCRISP APPLE, DICED

3 OUNCES PECORINO CHEESE, SHAVED

1. Make sure the chopped kale is very dry and place it in a large salad bowl. Pour 1 tablespoon lemon juice and ¼ teaspoon of the salt over the kale and massage the leaves gently for 4 to 5 minutes to tenderize them.

2. Combine the honey, remaining lemon juice, remaining 1 teaspoon salt, the pepper flakes, olive oil, and shallot in a Mason jar. Shake well.

3. Toss the kale with the pecans, dates, apple, and cheese. Add dressing to taste and toss to coat the kale thoroughly.

> **SOUTHERN SIMPLE:** Fresh kale is available all year but is best in the colder months. Store fresh kale in the coldest part of your fridge's crisper drawer.

> **SOUTHERN MOTHER:** Kale provides a good amount of folate, calcium, and iron.

CREAMY COCONUT FRUIT SALAD

That's right, I'm real Southern. Y'all can tell because miniature marshmallows in a salad don't even cause me to blink. In my travels, I've found marshmallows in salad to be more common when you get south of Louisville, Kentucky. This ambrosia recipe has made me a star on the potluck circuit, especially when I serve it anywhere outside the Southeast. Sour cream is whipped with a dash of coconut extract and sugar for the dressing, then folded into a combination of fresh and sweetened fruits. When the marshmallows lounge around in the fruit juices, getting all snuggled up next to the apricots, it's my favorite part of this salad.

Makes 6 servings

ONE 15-OUNCE CAN MANDARIN ORANGES, DRAINED

1½ CUPS DICED FRESH PINEAPPLE

1 CUP SEEDLESS RED GRAPES, HALVED

ONE 15.25-OUNCE CAN APRICOTS, DRAINED AND DICED

2 CUPS MINIATURE MARSHMALLOWS

1 CUP SWEETENED FLAKED COCONUT

¾ CUP SOUR CREAM, KEPT VERY COLD

½ TEASPOON COCONUT EXTRACT

2 TABLESPOONS SUGAR

1. Combine the oranges, pineapple, grapes, apricots, marshmallows, and coconut in a large bowl.

2. Using a very cold whisk and a very cold, large bowl, whip the sour cream, coconut extract, and sugar until fluffy.

3. Fold the fruit mixture into the sour cream mixture. Chill for at least 2 hours in the fridge and serve cold.

SOUTHERN SIMPLE: If you have never whipped sour cream, you might have found a new addition to many of your favorite dishes. It will whip up nicely if you make sure the sour cream and your bowl and whisk are cold, cold, cold.

SOUTHERN SIMPLE: Serve this make-ahead salad with Vacation Crabmeat Quiche (page 197) for a brunch that's done even before company comes.

My aunt Gail is one of the sweetest, most generous people I know. She never had children of her own, so she spoils the rest of us to no end. And we love it! Everyone is drawn to her—even the stray kittens and pups that somehow show up on her doorstep waiting for some of that special treatment. Aunt Gail loves salads of all sorts and this is one of her favorites.

SWEET POTATO CASSEROLE

You can put my mama's sweet potatoes up against anyone else's in the world! Anytime we have a family get-together, it's always "Barbara's got to bring the sweet potatoes!" I think she sprinkles fairy dust on top. There's just something about them that makes them extra special.

Makes 6 servings

6 TO 8 POUNDS SWEET POTATOES, ABOUT 4 CUPS WHEN COOKED AND MASHED

1½ STICKS BUTTER

¾ CUP MARSHMALLOW CRÈME (MOST OF A 7-OUNCE JAR)

¼ CUP EVAPORATED MILK

¼ CUP SUGAR

1 TEASPOON VANILLA EXTRACT

½ TEASPOON SALT

1 CUP SELF-RISING FLOUR

1 CUP PACKED LIGHT BROWN SUGAR

1. Preheat the oven to 350°F.

2. In a large pot of boiling water, cook the sweet potatoes until tender, about 30 minutes. Drain and return them to the pan to cool. Peel off the skin and mash the sweet potatoes with a potato masher.

3. Using an electric mixer, blend the sweet potatoes, ½ stick of the butter, the marshmallow crème, evaporated milk, sugar, vanilla, and salt. Spread the mixture evenly in a 9 x 13-inch baking dish.

4. Combine the flour, brown sugar, and remaining 1 stick butter in a medium bowl. You can use a pastry cutter to mix the topping if you like.

5. Sprinkle the topping over the sweet potatoes and bake until the topping is golden brown, about 40 minutes.

SOUTHERN MOTHER: The stand mixer, or "the Blister" as we call it in our house, is helpful not only to mix the ingredients together but also to catch the strings that come off the sweet potatoes, which should be discarded.

VACATION CRABMEAT QUICHE

Traveling down to the Gulf of Mexico is a favorite trip for our family. When we have a few days at the beach, I try to cook as much fresh Gulf seafood as I can. I reach for sweet blue crab on the first trip to the market. This quiche is easy to prepare in a vacation rental setting. A store-bought pie shell gets this anytime dish going, and the other ingredients are convenient when cooking away from home because they can all do double duty in another meal.

Makes one 9-inch pie

3 EGGS

½ CUP MAYONNAISE

2½ TABLESPOONS ALL-PURPOSE FLOUR

½ CUP MILK

1 TEASPOON SALT

½ TEASPOON FRESHLY GROUND BLACK PEPPER

⅓ CUP DICED BELL PEPPER

1 CUP CRABMEAT (SEE SOUTHERN SIMPLE)

½ CUP MINCED ONION

6 SLICES BACON, COOKED AND CRUMBLED

1 CUP GRATED CHEDDAR CHEESE

ONE 9-INCH STORE-BOUGHT PIE SHELL

1. Preheat the oven to 350°F.

2. Whisk the eggs lightly in a large bowl. Whisk in the mayonnaise, flour, milk, salt, and black pepper. Stir in the bell pepper, crabmeat, onion, and bacon.

3. Prick the pie shell 5 times. Sprinkle the grated Cheddar over the bottom of the crust. Pour the egg mixture on top of the cheese. Bake until the crust is golden brown, 40 to 45 minutes.

SOUTHERN SIMPLE: Crabmeat is sold "fresh," pasteurized, frozen, and canned. "Fresh" crabmeat is lightly cooked to release the meat from the shell. Pasteurized crabmeat goes through an additional cooking process to extend the shelf life. Frozen crabmeat has been cooked to remove it from the shell, then flash frozen. Canned crabmeat has been cooked and processed more than all the other choices. Blue crab is graded and sold according to the size of the chunks of meat. Jumbo lump crabmeat is the priciest, and I'd save that for a crab cocktail.

(continued)

For this recipe, look for crabmeat labeled backfin or lump. Backfin comes from the rear fin area and contains some large pieces of meat mixed with broken or smaller lumps. Be sure to carefully inspect crabmeat for any bits of shell or cartilage that may have been missed by the pickers before you add it to the recipe.

COASTAL CAROLINA SHRIMP AND CHEDDAR GRIT CAKES

One of the most gracious ladies I have had the pleasure to meet on my travels is award-winning cookbook author Nathalie Dupree. While I was visiting Charleston, South Carolina, Miss Nathalie taught me all about the regional classic Low Country dish shrimp and grits. Nathalie is a great hostess and inspired this dish. It's wonderful for sharing with guests in that casual coastal Carolina way.

Makes 4 to 6 servings

GRIT CAKES

OLIVE OIL, FOR THE BAKING DISH AND FOR BRUSHING

3½ CUPS MILK

2 GARLIC CLOVES, MINCED

1 CUP QUICK-COOKING GRITS

½ CUP GRATED SMOKED CHEDDAR CHEESE

½ TEASPOON SALT

¼ TEASPOON FRESHLY GROUND BLACK PEPPER

2 TABLESPOONS CHOPPED FRESH PARSLEY

SHRIMP

5 SLICES THICK-CUT BACON, CUT INTO SMALL PIECES

¼ CUP MINCED SHALLOTS

½ CUP HEAVY (WHIPPING) CREAM

ONE 10-OUNCE PACKAGE FROZEN CREAM CORN, THAWED

1 TEASPOON CREOLE-STYLE SEASONING, SUCH AS ZATARAIN'S

1 TABLESPOON FRESH THYME LEAVES

1 POUND LARGE (16/20 COUNT) SHRIMP, SHELLED AND DEVEINED, TAIL ON

2 GARLIC CLOVES, MINCED

SALT AND FRESHLY GROUND BLACK PEPPER

1. Make the grit cakes: Oil a 9-inch square glass baking dish.

2. Combine the milk and garlic in a medium saucepan and bring to a simmer over medium heat. Slowly whisk in the grits and cook, whisking, until very thick, about 5 minutes. Remove from the heat and whisk in the Cheddar until melted. Add the salt, pepper, and parsley. Pour into the dish and press plastic wrap directly onto the surface of the grits. Refrigerate the grits until firm, about 30 minutes.

(continued)

3. Preheat the broiler to high. Unmold the grits onto a cutting board and cut them into 9 squares. Lay the squares on a baking sheet, brush them with olive oil, and broil until golden brown and warmed through, 2 to 3 minutes per side. Keep them warm.

4. Meanwhile, make the shrimp: Cook the bacon until crispy in a large skillet over medium heat. Scoop out the bacon bits and set them on a paper towel to drain. Pour most of the drippings off but leave 2 tablespoons in the pan. Add the shallots and remaining garlic and cook, stirring, until translucent, about 2 minutes. Add the bacon, cream, cream corn, Creole seasoning, and thyme and stir. Add the shrimp and cook until opaque and cooked through, about 8 minutes. Season with salt and pepper to taste. Serve the shrimp and sauce on top of the grit cakes.

SOUTHERN SIMPLE: When you're purchasing fresh shrimp, Nathalie Dupree advises to look for a slightly red cast to the legs.

SOUTHERN SIMPLE: This recipe is great for entertaining. Make the grit cakes but hold off on broiling them, and prepare the topping up to the point when the shrimp are added. When your guests arrive, you'll just need to broil the grit cakes and add the shrimp to the reheated sauce and cook for 8 minutes. The guests will appreciate the culinary show, and you'll have time to actually visit with your company.

CRISPY TROUT CAKES

The Caney Fork River in Smith County, Tennessee, teems with rainbow, brown, and brook trout. I once got the chance to go fishing with expert fly fisherman David Hudnall when we were up that way. The flies David ties are truly wondrous little creations, each patterned using iridescent threads and festooned with the teeniest feathers. There's an art to the actual fly-fishing as well.

These crisp trout cakes work wonderfully as an appetizer and are a great centerpiece to a luncheon entrée salad.

Makes 4 servings

1 POUND TROUT, SKINNED, BONED, AND CUT INTO SMALL CHUNKS

½ CUP DICED RED BELL PEPPER

¼ CUP FINELY CHOPPED SCALLIONS

2 TABLESPOONS CHOPPED FRESH PARSLEY

1 TABLESPOON WHOLE-GRAIN MUSTARD

GRATED ZEST AND JUICE OF 1 LEMON (LEAVE A WEDGE FOR SQUEEZING)

1 EGG

1 CUP PANKO BREADCRUMBS

1 TEASPOON SALT, PLUS MORE FOR SPRINKLING

¼ TEASPOON FRESHLY GROUND BLACK PEPPER

VEGETABLE OIL, FOR SHALLOW-FRYING

1. Combine all the ingredients except the frying oil in a bowl and form 4 cakes. Cover the cakes and refrigerate for 20 minutes to firm.

2. When ready to cook, heat ¼ inch of vegetable oil in a large skillet over medium heat. Cook the cakes until deep golden brown, about 3 minutes per side. Drain the cakes on paper towels. Season with salt and squeeze the lemon wedge over the top.

SOUTHERN SIMPLE: If trout is not available, choose U.S. farm-raised catfish. Its mild flavor works really well in this recipe.

My husband treasures a rusty tin cigarette box that once belonged to his great-grandfather. The box is filled with the flies his granddaddy tied many years ago. We're saving these for Daisy's first trip to go fly-fishing with her daddy.

Down-Home Rockefeller: Baked Oysters with Creamed Turnip Greens

In my travels, when I find myself in a restaurant that touts its Oysters Rockefeller, I can't resist giving them a try. It's one of my all-time favorite dishes! This is my down-home version of that delicacy. I've changed out the watercress in the original dish for thinly sliced turnip greens and cook them in individual ramekins topped with the oysters. A quick grating of lemon zest and squeeze of juice when the oysters come out of the oven is all that is needed before they're served.

Makes 4 servings

4 SLICES SMOKED BACON, CUT INTO 2-INCH PIECES

2 TABLESPOONS BUTTER

1 CUP THINLY SLICED LEEKS

7 CUPS WASHED AND THINLY SLICED TURNIP GREENS (CUT INTO CHIFFONADE; SEE PAGE 206) OR ONE 16-OUNCE PACKAGE CHOPPED TURNIP GREENS

1½ CUPS HEAVY (WHIPPING) CREAM

1 TABLESPOON PLUS 1 TEASPOON HOT SAUCE

SALT AND FRESHLY GROUND BLACK PEPPER

2 DOZEN OYSTERS, ROUGHLY CHOPPED

GRATED ZEST AND JUICE OF 1 LEMON

1. Preheat the oven to 400°F.

2. Cook the bacon slices in a large skillet over medium-high heat until they start to render their fat, about 5 minutes. Add the butter and let it melt in with the bacon fat, then add the leeks and cook, stirring occasionally, for 5 minutes, or until they soften. Add the turnip greens and stir until they are wilted. Add the cream and hot sauce and season with salt and pepper to taste. Cover and simmer until very tender, 10 to 15 minutes.

3. Spoon the mixture into four 8-ounce ramekins set on a rimmed baking sheet and divide the chopped oysters evenly on top. Cover the ramekins with lids or foil and bake for 5 minutes, or until the oysters are warmed through. Top the oysters with lemon zest and a bit of lemon juice and serve immediately.

(continued)

SOUTHERN SIMPLE: I cut the turnip greens into a chiffonade, the French culinary term that means "made of rags." To do this, roll the greens like a big cigar and cut across the roll in ⅛-inch slices. I used to watch my papa roll his own cigars, and I was always fascinated at how tight he got those little guys! Turns out that came in handy!

SOUTHERN SIMPLE: Look for tubs of pasteurized oysters in the seafood section, shuck your own, or smile nicely at the person selling the oysters and ask them to do it for you.

SOUTHERN MOTHER: I like to serve this dish with Crostini and Black-Eyed Pea Puree (page 105) on New Year's Day to ensure good luck and prosperity—not that I'm superstitious! But it never fails: if I'm not with my mama and daddy on New Year's Day, Mama always calls to check and make sure I've had my required servings of turnip greens and black-eyed peas. If the answer is ever "No," I get a good scolding. You don't want to disappoint Mama!

LOW COUNTRY BOIL

As crazy as it sounds, when I get time off from touring on the bus, one of my favorite things to do is spend a week in a camper. My folks always took us camping as a family, and a few years back they bought a camper. Then over the years all our family ended up with campers. All totaled we've got fourteen folks in four campers. When we go down to a campground on a lake in South Carolina for a week each summer, we line all the campers up in a row and have the best time bopping back and forth between them and the communal fire ring.

My mumu is always in charge of breakfast because she's the earliest riser. We'll pack a shore lunch for a midday break from inner-tubing and waterskiing. Then when we're all back at home base and the sun is thinking about setting, all the men put on a Low Country boil. There are a lot of games and hijinks while the big pot boils and slowly fills with all the ingredients.

A Low Country boil builds up as it cooks. First the hot peppers, celery, onion, and seasonings go in the pot. Once those flavors have infused the water, the slow-to-cook potatoes are added. Next comes smoked sausage and corn on the cob. Then, last but not least, the shrimp are added to the well-seasoned liquid to cook for just a couple of minutes. The whole shebang gets a luscious roll in butter and another shot of spice and it's dumped out right down the middle of the table for everyone to elbow up and dig right in! Now, that, my friend, is living!

Makes 6 servings

2 LARGE JALAPEÑOS, QUARTERED LENGTHWISE

3 CELERY STALKS, CUT INTO THIRDS

1 LARGE ONION, CUT INTO 8 PIECES

5 GARLIC CLOVES, SMASHED

2 TABLESPOONS OLD BAY SEASONING, PLUS MORE FOR SERVING

1 POUND NEW POTATOES

1 POUND SMOKED PORK SAUSAGE, CUT INTO 2-INCH PIECES

2 EARS OF CORN, SHUCKED AND QUARTERED

1 POUND LARGE (16/20 COUNT) SHELL-ON SHRIMP

4 TABLESPOONS (½ STICK) BUTTER

2 TABLESPOONS HOT SAUCE

2 TABLESPOONS CHOPPED FRESH PARSLEY

(continued)

1. Combine the jalapeños, celery, onion, garlic, 1 tablespoon of the Old Bay, and 10 cups water in a large pot. Bring to a boil over high heat. Add the potatoes and cook for 5 minutes. Reduce the heat to medium, add the sausage to the pot, and cook for 15 minutes. Add the corn and cook until the potatoes are cooked through, about 10 minutes. Stir in the shrimp and cook until the shrimp are opaque throughout, about 2 minutes.

2. Reserving 1 cup of the cooking liquid, drain the shrimp mixture. Set the shrimp mixture aside.

3. Using the same pot, combine the butter, the remaining 1 tablespoon Old Bay, the hot sauce, parsley, and reserved cooking liquid and set over medium heat. When the butter is melted, return the shrimp mixture to the pot and stir well to coat all the ingredients with the butter sauce.

4. Dump the Low Country boil onto a table lined with butcher paper or newspaper. Serve with more Old Bay if desired.

SOUTHERN SIMPLE: To make your own spice blend for a Low Country boil, combine 3 tablespoons paprika, 2 tablespoons kosher salt, 2 tablespoons garlic powder, 1 tablespoon onion powder, 2 teaspoons cayenne pepper, 1 teaspoon dill seeds, 1 teaspoon dried thyme, 1 teaspoon dried oregano, and 1 teaspoon freshly ground black pepper. Start with that and play with it until you get it just how you like it. Store the mix in an airtight container.

SOUTHERN MOTHER: To aid in the cleanup following a Low Country boil, I pick up a disposable plastic party tablecloth from the dollar store, then I lay butcher paper or newspaper on top. When the carnage is over, the whole lot can be rolled up and thrown away.

MAPLE MONTE CRISTO SANDWICH

I am a grilled sandwich fanatic! This may be my crowning achievement in sandwich making. Think of French toast and smoky bacon. Then imagine maple dressing, melted Gruyère cheese, and hickory-smoked turkey sandwiched between the two. Now envision a dusting of powdered sugar gently falling across the golden-brown sandwich. Stars and garters! This is my favorite sandwich.

Makes 4 sandwiches

MAPLE MAYO

½ CUP MAYONNAISE

1½ TABLESPOONS BROWN SUGAR

2 TABLESPOONS MAPLE SYRUP

⅛ TEASPOON SALT

SANDWICHES

8 SLICES BACON

4 EGGS

⅓ CUP MILK

1 TEASPOON SALT

¼ TEASPOON FRESHLY GROUND BLACK PEPPER

8 SLICES TOASTING BREAD

16 THIN SLICES DELI TURKEY (10 TO 12 OUNCES)

8 SLICES GRUYÈRE CHEESE

2 TABLESPOONS POWDERED SUGAR

1. Make the maple mayo: Mix all the ingredients together in a small bowl.

2. Make the sandwiches: Cook the bacon in a skillet until crispy. Drain the bacon on paper towels. Pour off all but 2 tablespoons of bacon fat from the pan.

3. Beat the eggs in a shallow dish. Whisk in the milk, salt, and pepper.

4. Build the sandwiches by spreading mayo on each slice of bread. Use 4 slices turkey, 2 slices bacon, and 2 slices Gruyère in each sandwich and press the sandwich together lightly.

5. Heat the skillet of bacon fat over medium heat.

6. Dip each side of the sandwich into the egg mixture. Cook each sandwich in the skillet until toasted, 4 to 5 minutes per side. Sprinkle the sandwiches with powdered sugar and serve.

SOUTHERN SIMPLE: The maple mayonnaise used on this sandwich is also a nice addition to the Happy, Happy Grilled Turkey Burgers with Maple Caramelized Onions (page 171).

SOUTHERN MOTHER: This sandwich and a plate of Sweet Potato Oven Fries (page 157) is an ideal late-night dinner.

Rosemary Ham and Brie Sandwiches with Plum Jus

I like to dunk. This thick-sliced ham, plum, and Brie sandwich is served up with a tart plum sauce for dipping.

Makes 4 sandwiches

1 tablespoon olive oil

2 teaspoons minced fresh rosemary

One 16-ounce fully cooked smoked ham steak

4 ciabatta rolls, split horizontally and toasted

1 plum, thinly sliced

8 slices Brie cheese

A handful of mixed baby salad greens

Mayonnaise, to taste

Dijon mustard, to taste

Plum Jus (recipe follows)

1. Preheat the oven to 350°F.

2. Heat the olive oil and rosemary in a medium skillet over medium-high heat for 1 minute. Add the ham steak and cook for 2 minutes on each side to heat through. Remove the ring bone and cut the ham into 4 equal pieces.

3. On the roll bottoms, layer the ham, plum, and Brie. Top with some salad greens. Spread some mayonnaise and Dijon mustard on the roll tops. Close the sandwiches and serve them with the Plum Jus for dipping.

Plum Jus

Makes about 1 cup

1½ POUNDS PLUMS (ABOUT 6), ROUGHLY CHOPPED

½ CUP SUGAR

2 TABLESPOONS BALSAMIC VINEGAR

Combine all the ingredients in a medium saucepan and simmer on low heat until the plums soften and break down, 20 to 25 minutes. Pour the mixture into a sieve and strain into a bowl. Reserve the "jus" liquid and discard the skins.

PAULA'S HOUSE FULL OF FOLKS BREAKFAST CASSEROLE

As far as traditions go, I'm as corny as they come. I get it from my mama. Every year she sets out to find matching pajamas for the family. Not just the children, mind you, the whole family. She starts worrying about it in the fall, and by Christmas Eve she's pulled it all together—fourteen sets (and counting) of matching pajamas in sizes that change each year as the children grow. It started with her first grandchildren, then it grew to the silly tradition of all of us wearing matching pajamas. We all change into our matching regalia and gather around the tree, and my daddy reads the Christmas story from the Gospel of Luke. That's incredibly special! Then we set out cookies and eggnog for Santa and reindeer food for Rudolph. It's always very late by then, and we scamper to get the kiddos to bed. They all sleep together upstairs piled in beds and bundled on pallets on the floor, and the grown-ups tend to "things."

Christmas morning, when the children are clamoring to go downstairs, the grown-ups stop them on the stairway and make them line up, stair-step fashion, youngest to oldest. We take a bazillion pictures, and after much pleading on their part, we turn them loose to see what Santa Claus has brought. We always have Paula's Breakfast Casserole and then lounge around all day in slippers and our matching pajamas. My favorite day of the year!

Makes 6 servings

ONE 8-OUNCE PACKAGE REFRIGERATED CRESCENT ROLLS

1 POUND LOOSE BREAKFAST SAUSAGE, COOKED AND DRAINED

2 CUPS SHREDDED COLBY JACK CHEESE

6 EGGS

2 CUPS MILK

1 TEASPOON SALT

½ TEASPOON FRESHLY GROUND BLACK PEPPER

1 TABLESPOON CHOPPED FRESH OREGANO

1 TABLESPOON CHOPPED FRESH PARSLEY

1. Preheat the oven to 350°F. Grease a 9 x 13-inch baking pan.

2. Unroll and spread the crescent rolls to cover the bottom of the pan. Evenly spread the cooked sausage and Jack cheese on top.

3. Whisk together the eggs and milk in a medium bowl. Mix in the salt, pepper, oregano, and parsley and pour the egg mixture over the sausage. Bake, uncovered, until golden brown, 40 to 45 minutes.

SOUTHERN SIMPLE: To get a head start on this breakfast dish, combine the cooled cooked sausage with the cheese and herbs and seasonings and refrigerate the mixture. The next day, when you're ready to bake, just add the eggs and milk and pour the mixture over the crescent dough.

LAZY WOMAN'S STRAWBERRY PIE

It's not like a lazy woman would be making a pie in the first place, and it's an 8-inch square, so the whole name of this warm strawberry dessert is ridiculous. Makes me love it all the more! This recipe comes together in a flash and is perfect for making away from home. Five ingredients, one dish, and three minutes to oven time. That's how a "lazy" woman on the run gets dessert done!

Makes 6 servings

8 TABLESPOONS (1 STICK) BUTTER

1 CUP SUGAR

1 CUP SELF-RISING FLOUR

¾ CUP MILK

ONE 10-OUNCE PACKAGE FROZEN SWEETENED STRAWBERRIES, THAWED

1. Preheat the oven to 350°F.

2. Place the butter in an 8-inch square glass baking dish. Place the dish in the oven to melt the butter.

3. Meanwhile, combine the sugar and flour in a medium bowl. Add the milk and stir until well combined.

4. Pour the mixture into the pan on top of the melted butter, but do not stir. Pour the strawberries over the top. Again, do not stir! After all, this *is* a lazy woman's pie!

5. Bake for 45 minutes, or until the top is golden brown.

SOUTHERN SIMPLE: Serve this "pie" warm with vanilla frozen yogurt.

SOUTHERN SIMPLE: For a tangy version, use sweetened frozen raspberries, and drizzle it with chocolate sauce when it comes out of the oven.

SOUTHERN SIMPLE: This is one of those recipes that friends pass around. Give this easy recipe to a friend on a note card right after you have served it to them. That's what true friends do . . .

When I was pregnant with Daisy, I thought a lot about what my child would be drawn to. At times I secretly hoped that she would want to be a teacher or doctor or vet and have very little inkling for the pursuit of music, only because the music business can be a real heartbreaker and very difficult. Well, I can't tell you how very far off I was! My child has been writing songs since she was three! Her first one was called "Strawberry Shortcake Rocks My World"! She'll sing and dance for anyone who will listen and watch, and I *love* it! To see how music affects her—and how she affects others through her love for it—makes me an incredibly proud mommy, and I'll be her biggest fan whether she's standing on a classroom stage or on the world's biggest musical stage. Her love of music is infectious and beautiful, and it's in her blood.

CHOCOLATE PUDDING

I strive for the road to feel as much like home as possible for our family, so I try to take along as much homemade goodness as I can. One day Daisy suggested we make this pudding, place it in individual containers, and take them on the bus to share. What a great idea! Everybody had their own portion, and it was a nice little cozy dose of home.

Makes 4 servings

1½ CUPS SUGAR

¼ CUP UNSWEETENED COCOA POWDER

5 TABLESPOONS CORNSTARCH

ONE 12-OUNCE CAN EVAPORATED MILK

3 CUPS MILK

PINCH OF SALT

1 TEASPOON VANILLA EXTRACT

1 TABLESPOON BUTTER

Combine the sugar, cocoa powder, and cornstarch in a medium saucepan. Stir in the evaporated milk and fresh milk and bring the mixture to a boil over low heat. Cook, stirring occasionally, until the pudding has thickened, about 5 minutes. Remove the pudding from the heat, add the salt, vanilla, and butter, and stir to mix well. Serve the pudding warm or refrigerate it.

SOUTHERN SIMPLE: To keep pudding from forming a thick skin on top, press plastic wrap directly on the surface of the pudding.

SOUTHERN MOTHER: When my mama makes this, she stirs everything together well, then cooks it in the microwave for 5 minutes. Stirs well again. Cooks for another 5 minutes. Stirs and checks the consistency. If it needs more time to thicken, she'll cook it in shorter increments, stir, and cook till it's done.

SOUTHERN MOTHER: I like to serve this intensely chocolaty pudding with whipped cream and a variety of candy sprinkles, like chopped Butterfingers, Hershey bars, or peppermint chocolate.

CRAZY DAISY'S SQUARES

Daisy and I are crafters. Although I'm not very good at it, we both love an afternoon of arts and crafts. Once we were visiting a "paint your own" pottery studio. Daisy made a plate for her daddy that said, "My daddy eats dessert first!" She was so tickled with herself for coming up with that to paint on his plate.

She loves to lend a hand making these simple chocolate and butterscotch treats. These are so easy that they're perfect for making in a camper or in a kitchenette.

Makes 9 squares

COOKING SPRAY

8 TABLESPOONS (1 STICK) BUTTER, MELTED

1½ CUPS GRAHAM CRACKER CRUMBS

1 CUP SEMISWEET CHOCOLATE CHIPS

1 CUP BUTTERSCOTCH BAKING CHIPS

1 CUP SWEETENED FLAKED COCONUT

1 CUP PECAN PIECES

ONE 14-OUNCE CAN SWEETENED CONDENSED MILK

1. Preheat the oven to 325°F. Coat an 8-inch square glass baking dish with cooking spray.

2. Combine the melted butter and graham cracker crumbs in a medium bowl. Press the mixture into the bottom of the dish.

3. Combine the chocolate chips, butterscotch chips, coconut, and pecans in a medium bowl. Sprinkle the mixture over the crumb bottom. Pour the sweetened condensed milk over the morsels and bake until the coconut is browned, 20 to 25 minutes. Remove from the oven and cool. Cut into squares.

SOUTHERN SIMPLE: I'm a dark chocolate fan. When I make these quick bars for a hostess gift or to take to a potluck, I use a combination of dark chocolate chips and mint baking chips in place of the butterscotch chips in this recipe.

SOUTHERN MOTHER: Once these bars are completely cooled, wrap them individually for a lunch-box treat. These bars also make a great treat for a new mom!

DAISY PEARL MAKES AN APPEARANCE

It was one hot summer! I was great with child, three and a half weeks before my due date, and we were on tour with Martina McBride. A lot of the shows were outdoors. I guess that heat proved too much for my little bun in the oven—either that or she was just showing her very busy, outgoing personality from the get-go! We had had a couple of days off and were home just in time to fly back out to Phoenix, Arizona. I had a pretty bad upper respiratory infection with a cough at the time, and I was on antibiotics. We flew out and did the show and as soon as it was over, I went to my bunk on the bus to lie down. It was about 11 P.M.

A couple of hours later I was suddenly "awakened." Oh Gussie, I started shaking uncontrollably. I told my husband, who was on the road with us, and we called my nurse. Because of my sickness and cough, we were all hoping my cough had caused me to "awaken." (I don't know how to say that my water broke without saying it. I guess I said it!)

We were still parked at the venue and were supposed to leave momentarily for Las Vegas for the next night's show. We told only our bus driver about the little incident, and he found the nearest hospital. I remember walking off the bus saying to him, "We'll just get checked out and be right back."

Well, I never went back to the bus! As soon as I was checked by the nurse, she said, "Honey, you aren't going anywhere! You're in labor!" What a shock! Oh Lord, this can't happen! We have two more weeks of shows left on this tour, and then we have another week and a half to be home and get everything perfectly ready for our baby! We're nowhere close to home! We have no family in Arizona! My doctor isn't here and *my mama is 2,000 miles away*!!! What in the world!

Our driver went out to the bus to wake up Karen, who was in a deep sleep by this time. She was as shocked as we were. She came into the hospital and stayed for a while, then went back out to the bus to sleep. The bus stayed in the hospital parking lot that night. Jimi and Phillip came in with Karen the next morning, and we visited until they had to leave to drive to Las Vegas, because the show must go on!

Right at showtime, at 7 P.M. on July 27, 2007, Daisy Pearl Schlapman was born. We named her after two of her great-grandmothers.

It was the most beautiful moment of my life. Because my sister-in-law Michele lives in California and was the closest relative to Phoenix, she flew in and made it just in time for the birth. It was great to have her there. Steve needed her. She gave him someone to announce "It's a girl!" to. She's had four children of her own, so she was so much help in my first hours as a new mom. She stayed overnight and went back home the next morning.

My sweet hubby and I spent the next three days falling in love with our little surprise all alone in Phoenix. He was left to make tons of phone calls, run around buying baby necessities, and take care of Daisy and me. My doctor didn't want us to fly, so we had a bus come pick us up. Just as we were packing and gearing up for a daunting thirty-three-hour bus ride home with a four-day-old baby, into the hospital walked my mama! I burst into tears. My hubby had arranged for her to fly out so that she could ride the bus home with us. That was the sweetest gift I've ever been given. I don't know how we would have made it home without her!

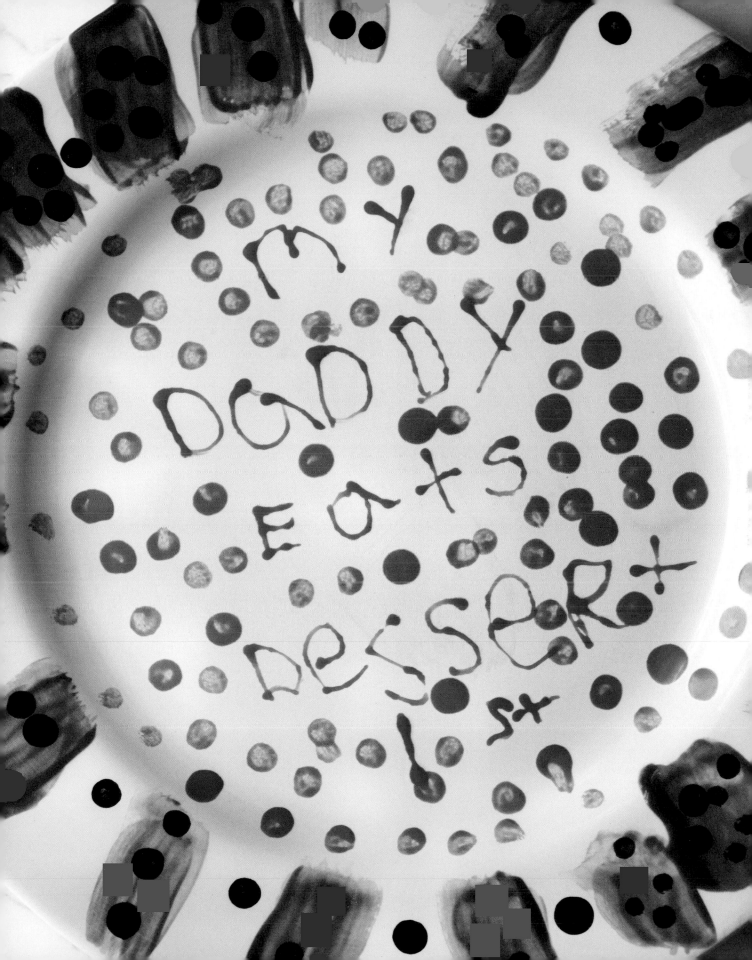

DREAMSICLE PUNCH

This punch tastes like summer vacation. I love to serve this when we're poolside, or wish we were.

Makes about 14 cups

ONE 2-LITER BOTTLE ORANGE SODA

ONE 14-OUNCE CAN SWEETENED CONDENSED MILK

1 QUART (32 OUNCES) PINEAPPLE JUICE

½ GALLON ORANGE SHERBET

Pour the orange soda, sweetened condensed milk, and pineapple juice into a large punch bowl or pitcher. Stir. Scoop the sherbet into the punch and serve.

SOUTHERN SIMPLE: This is also wonderful with lemon-lime soda and lime sherbet.

SOUTHERN MOTHER: I like to serve this from an insulated drink dispenser. Fill the dispenser with ice for 30 minutes, remove the ice, and mix the punch in the chilled dispenser.

Skinny Southern Sweet Tea

I like my tea like I like my tea. When you're on the road, it can be hard to find a good sweet tea! Those bottled concoctions just don't cut it. When I head out on the road, I make sure I have this sweet, sweet mint and citrus tea.

Makes 2 quarts

4 FAMILY-SIZE TEA BAGS

1 CUP SUGAR

¾ CUP SPLENDA

2 LEMONS, SLICED

2 LIMES, SLICED

5 MINT SPRIGS

1. Place the tea bags and 2 quarts water in a large saucepan over medium-high heat. Bring to a boil. Remove from the heat and steep for 20 minutes.

2. Pour into a gallon jar or jug and add the sugar and Splenda. Stir until the sugar is dissolved. Fill the rest of the gallon jar with cold water. Add the lemon and lime slices and mint sprigs. Serve over ice.

SOUTHERN SIMPLE: If I've got a thirsty bunch and am in a hurry for my tea to be done, I'll add ice to the hot tea after it steeps to cool it down quickly, then cold water to fill up the gallon jar. That way the ice won't melt and water down the tea when you pour it over the ice. Watered-down sweet tea is not good sweet tea!

ACKNOWLEDGMENTS

I love cookbooks! Sometimes when I find a little spare time, I just want to crawl up in the sunshine with a good cookbook and a glass of sweet tea. I really never thought I would write a cookbook, but I'm so grateful to HarperCollins for the unique opportunity. They have allowed me to show you just who I am, barefoot in the kitchen. Thank you, Cassie Jones and Kara Zauberman, for being dream editors and for letting me be me.

Were it not for some very generous and patient loved ones, this book would not exist. First of all, Schlappy and Daisy, thank you for understanding when I would have a dozen test dishes going on in the kitchen and yet we had to have cold cereal for supper. Daisy, thank you for turning my tears to laughter when things went way wrong. You are pure sunshine. Schlappy, thank you for sweetly kissing me on the head when you walked through the kitchen as I was frantically playing mad scientist and for letting me turn your willing palate from "refined Northern" to "down-home Southern." You two are my life!

Mama, how in the world would I have made it through this without your ciphering of all those heirloom recipes where you just "add a pinch of this and a dab of that"! Every time I called you in a panic, you said, "Don't worry, I'll get right on it," and you grabbed the keys and ran straight to the grocery store—or sent Daddy!

With a schedule like mine, it takes a village to pull something like this off! Kelly Jarrell, there's no better liaison and cheerleader! Thank you for believing in me whenever I doubted, and for knowing me so well that you can speak for me. Also, thank you for being such a lover of my Tried-and-True Almond Pound Cake. I'll make it for you till I'm too old to stand!

Shaina Burrell, everybody needs a "Shaina Baina"! You're like the concierge of my life! I would be a disaster without your help. Thank you caring about all the details, for being the little ribbon on my finger that gently reminds me of the many things I've forgotten, for grocery shopping for me, for cleaning up my sinkfuls of dishes, and for being my behind-the-scenes, pull-everything-together girl! Thank you also for being my stylist on this shoot. You're incredibly special!

Megan Pepke, thank you for coming to my aid and being my sous-chef in the eleventh hour, with a spoon in one hand and a math book in the other!

Ms. Brenda Fairchild, it was an honor to have an incredible cook like you testing some of these recipes.

Karen Fairchild, Jimi Westbrook, and Phillip Sweet, thank you for believing in and enabling my passion for cooking. You have been my skinny guinea pigs over the years, and you've graciously tried every dish I brought to you, even the ones that were kind of like a bad song. When I lost my first husband, Steve, whom I so loved to cook for, in tears I asked, "Who am I going to cook for now?!" Karen, you took me in your arms and said, "Me!" I'll never forget that moment. I love cooking for y'all!

Jason Owen, thank you for dreaming as big as I do. You are the best manager, protector, friend, comrade, gladiator—I could go on and on—a girl could ask for! Thank you for bringing out the best parts of me and for hiding all the rest! I owe you a lifetime of cookies!

Cait Hoyt, when I first met you, I thought, what a gorgeous, adorable lady. Then I saw you work! Wow! You know how take on a crusade and make dreams come true! Thank you!

Monica Hutchison, you've been like my favorite professor. You're the only chef school I've ever had. You've taught me so much, and it's a joy to partner with you in the kitchen. Thank you for all the testing of these recipes.

Martha, oh Martha, when we set out to find someone to help me put this book together, I stopped in my tracks when I heard your name, both because of your great success and reputation in this field and because you're so perfectly Southern! I thank God that our country-girl paths crossed. Thank you for finding my voice, for leading me so smoothly though uncharted waters, and for being the calm, sane one—when I was running around like a chicken with my head cut off. You're incredible at what you do! It's been an absolute pleasure to work with you on this labor of love.

Well, I don't wake up looking like this! It takes some very early mornings, false eyelashes, heavy curl cream, and one talented hair and makeup artist. Neil Robison, thank you for getting me all gussied up and for making me feel pretty, all the while being a great friend.

I can write out these recipes, but a cookbook without photos would be like cookies without milk! Our photography team was stellar! Heather Anne Thomas, as soon as I met you, I knew we would best fast friends. You have such a pleasant spirit and put the whole gang at ease. It was an absolute pleasure to have you and your crew in our home. You brought the food to life on these pages! It's beautiful and cozy and makes my mouth water! Michael Pederson, what a sweetheart you are! You prepared the food so gloriously and took such care to do it just how I had in mind. Kevin Green and Dustin Busby, thank you for your generous and meticulous "sous cheffing" to make the food look absolutely perfect. Thank you, Brittany Payne, for your help in pulling it all off. Zane Jernigan, thanks for turning out those gorgeous photos and for graciously letting me and my wishy-washy self see the same photos over and over again until I could make a decision. Mary Clayton Carl, please come live with me and make my house look like a photo shoot every day! You took the time to learn my taste spot-on. It was like you saw the whole concept through my eyes. You are my decorating hero!

And from Martha—a hearty, heartfelt thank-you to Robin Ramone Rushing and Jayne Jane Kennedy for fielding late-night calls, issuing sound advice, and being great pals.

UNIVERSAL CONVERSION CHART

Oven temperature equivalents

250°F = 120°C

275°F = 135°C

300°F = 150°C

325°F = 160°C

350°F = 180°C

375°F = 190°C

400°F = 200°C

425°F = 220°C

450°F = 230°C

475°F = 240°C

500°F = 260°C

Measurement equivalents

Measurements should always be level unless directed otherwise

⅛ teaspoon = 0.5 ml

¼ teaspoon = 1 ml

½ teaspoon = 2 ml

1 teaspoon = 5 ml

1 tablespoon = 3 teaspoons = ½ fluid ounce = 15 ml

2 tablespoons = ⅛ cup = 1 fluid ounce = 30 ml

4 tablespoons = ¼ cup = 2 fluid ounces = 60 ml

5⅓ tablespoons = ⅓ cup = 3 fluid ounces = 80 ml

8 tablespoons = ½ cup = 4 fluid ounces = 120 ml

10⅔ tablespoons = ⅔ cup = 5 fluid ounces = 160 ml

12 tablespoons = ¾ cup = 6 fluid ounces = 180 ml

16 tablespoons = 1 cup = 8 fluid ounces = 240 ml

RECIPES BY CATEGORY

INDEX

NOTE: Page references in *italics* refer to photos of recipes.

cheese. *see also* cream cheese
    in Asparagus Wrapped in Leaves, 150, *151*
    Cheddar Bacon Biscuits, 78–79, *79*
    Coastal Carolina Shrimp and Cheddar Grit
        Cakes, *200,* 201–202
    Collard Green Grilled Cheese, 68–69, *69*
    Cookie Press Cheese Straws, 107, *108*
    Creamy Smoked Mac and Cheese, 162–163,
        163
    Fruit and Cheese Kebabs, *108,* 109
    Grilled Watermelon with Goat Cheese and
        Prosciutto, 110, *111*
    in Josh's Chicken Alfredo, 164–165
    in Layered Salad, *6,* 7
    in Maple Monte Cristo Sandwich, 210–211, *211*
    in Mother's Day Asparagus Casserole, 118–
        120, *119*
    Papa's Peaches and Cottage Cheese, 9
    Parmesan Baked Tomatoes, 153
    in Pineapple Casserole, 191
    Roasted Figs with Goat Cheese and Vanilla
        Honey, 176–177, *177*
    Rosemary Ham and Brie Sandwiches with
        Plum Jus, 213–214
chicken
    Chicken and Hash Brown Casserole, 166
    Chicken and Herb White Pizza, 70–71
    Josh's Chicken Alfredo, 164–165
    Kimberly's Chicken and Dumplings, 30–31
    Make-Ahead Chicken and Rice, 27
    Mama's Chicken Biscuit Pie, 167–168, *169*
    in Manly Man Brunswick Stew, 16
    Simply Southern Fried Chicken, *24,* 25, *26*
    Slow-Cooker Chicken Quesadillas, 106
    in Southern Dressing and Gravy, 32–33
    in Three-Alarm Enchiladas, 72–73
chocolate
    Chocolate Cherry Cola Cake, 134–136, *135*
    Chocolate Pudding, 219
    in Christmas Coffee Punch, 59
    in Crazy Daisy's Squares, 220, *221*
    in Girlfriend S'mores, 94
    in Schlapp Happy Bars, 86, *87*
Christmas Coffee Punch, 59
citrus
    Citrus Cake with Lime Glaze, *82,* 83–84

Citrus Salad with Poppy Seed Dressing, *146,* 147
    Dreamsicle Punch, 225
    Strawberry Limeade, 187
    Sweet Orange Rolls, 178
Coastal Carolina Shrimp and Cheddar Grit
    Cakes, *200,* 201–202
coconut
    in Crazy Daisy's Squares, 220, *221*
    Creamy Coconut Fruit Salad, 194–195, *195*
    Friendly Coconut Pie, 88
    Grandmother's Coconut Pudding, 56–58, *57*
Coleslaw, Golden Delicious, *4,* 5
Collard Green Grilled Cheese, 68–69, *69*
Cookie Press Cheese Straws, 107, *108*
corn
    Coastal Carolina Shrimp and Cheddar Grit
        Cakes, *200,* 201–202
    Donna Schlapman's Corn Casserole, 22–23
    Grilled Creamed Corn, 156
    Pepper Jelly-Buttered Corn Summer Spread,
        154, *155*
cornbread
    Blueberry Cornbread Cupcakes, *80,* 80–81, *81*
    Grandmother Burrell's Mexican Cornbread, 40
    Hush Puppies, 42, 43
    in Southern Dressing and Gravy, 32–33
Country-Fried Steak and Milk Gravy, 37
Country Low Boil, 207–208, *209*
Crabmeat Quiche, Vacation, 197–198, *199*
Crazy Daisy's Squares, 220, *221*
cream cheese
    in Cucumber Tea Sandwiches, 8
    frosting for Black Walnut Cake, 182–184, *183*
    frosting for Hummingbird Cake, 137–138,
        138, 139
    in Slow-Cooker Chicken Quesadillas, 106
    in Southwest Tortilla Roll-Ups, 126
    in Vidalia Onion Dip, 102–103
Creamy Coconut Fruit Salad, 194–195, *195*
Creamy Smoked Mac and Cheese, 162–163, *163*
Crispy Trout Cakes, 203
Crostini and Black-Eyed Pea Puree, *104,* 105
cucumber
    Cucumber and Mint Soup, 112
    Cucumber and Tomato Salad, 66, *66, 67*
    Cucumber Tea Sandwiches, 8